# Introduction

*"Food is a passion. Food is love."*

Hector Elizondo

If you have always wanted to start canning at home but did not know how to start or what to do, then keep reading…this is the book for you!

You see, canning is not very difficult once you know what it involves. Even if you have never tried your hand at canning, it is easier than you might think. The first step to getting started with canning at home is to understand what pressure canning is, and the simple but important steps to be followed. Once you do this, you can start enjoying your favorite foods with your whole family all year long. Pressure canning is a food preservation process that involves using a special appliance called a pressure canner to seal the contents within a jar. From wild game, poultry, and beef to soups and stews and vegetarian ingredients, lots of different foods can be canned. All you need to do is understand what pressure canning is and how it works.

The concept of canning is nothing new and it has been around for decades. That said, with modern advancements and development, canning has become easier than ever before. It is also an incredibly efficient, safe, and practical means of preserving tasty meals in a jar. By using the different recipes given in this book, you can quickly rustle up healthy and filling meals. This book will also introduce you to the basic process of pressure canning, the equipment and tools involved in it, and an understanding of how this process works. It will also introduce you to a variety of factors that influence pressure canning. Once you are armed with all this information, you will be introduced to the different steps to be followed to start canning food at home.

In this book, you will learn about preparing meals in a jar and learning to can different types of foods. Whether it is meats, vegetables, or even stews and soups, they can be canned. So, do not stifle your creativity and instead, let it run wild. With the right safety information, practice, and patience, you can become a pro at canning within no time!

Are you wondering how I know all this? Well, I believe a little introduction is needed. Hello, my name is Linda Johnson and I have been canning for as long as I can remember. I grew up on a beautiful farm in rural Kansas. From a young age, I have been interested in gardening, farming, canning, food preserving, horse riding, and walking. I am not just passionate about canning but love sharing the goodies with my loving family and other loved ones. I am primarily a homemaker and a mother but I certainly know my way around the farm too.

I started sharing my tips and tricks for canning with others along with my preferred recipes. All the positive feedback I started receiving motivated me to compile my knowledge and experience into this book. I can imagine how intimidating canning might seem to a beginner. Well, you do not have to worry because I have got you covered. In this book, I will introduce you to everything you need to learn as a beginner. The information shared will ensure you aren't unknowingly following any unsafe canning practices. I believe canning is one of the best means to preserve food and avoid food wastage. And I am certain you can become an excellent canner within no time! Canning is extremely useful and simple to do once you get the hang of it. You can consume healthy and wholesome convenience food without any artificial preservatives. Also, this is more economical than any store-bought variant.

Even if you are just getting started, this book will act as your guide every step of the way. The tried and tested recipes given, coupled with simple instructions will turn you into a canning pro within no time! You will discover helpful information needed for creating perfect food storage options.

If you are ready to jump into the world of home canning, then there is no time like the present to get started!

# Chapter 1:
# Pressure Canning 101

*"Food is a necessary component to life. People can live without Renoir, Mozart, Gaudi, Beckett, but they cannot live without food."*

Grant Achatz

What is the first thing that pops into your head when you hear the words pressure canner? Chances are you think about a stovetop cooking pan with a lid and a noisy whistle. Well, you are probably thinking of a pressure cooker and not a canner. Chances are we most commonly use these two words as synonyms, but they are not. Even though they share some similarities, they don't refer to the same kitchen equipment. Usually, pressure cookers are used for cooking large cuts of meat quickly. These cooking appliances are like large saucepans. On the other hand, pressure canners are not meant for processing or cooking food but instead storing them through a process known as canning. The jars with food should be placed in the pressure canner and the pressure within it helps seal the jars. Usually, pressure canners are much larger than a cooker and can hold anywhere between 7 and 24 jars at any point.

Pressure canning is a wonderful technique used for food preservation using special kitchen equipment known as a pressure canner. This process helps extend the shelf-life of certain cooked foods. A pressure canner is a large pot with a lid that snugly fits it. It also has a weighted or a dial gauge to check the pressure building up within the pot. The added pressure created within helps sterilize the jars and ensure the food within them is pathogen-free.

I could write a whole book on Pressure Canning 101 basics and safety. In fact. I have! It's called **"Pressure Canning Without the Danger** - Your Comprehensive Guide to Safely Using Your Pressure Canner. With Tips, Tricks, and USDA Guidelines to Help You Use Your Pressure Canner Without Risks!". I encourage you to read it as it covers in much greater detail the topics I write about in this chapter.

# Brands and Types of Pressure Canners

When it comes to pressure canners, there are two brands that dominate the market, All-American and Presto. Both All-American and Presto pressure canners have their pros and cons. Ultimately, it is the customer's decision on what model makes them feel most comfortable.

All-American pressure canners come in a variety of sizes, which is perfect for people who plan on making large batches at a time. Their largest size will can 19 quart jars at a time, while their smallest holds only four. With this variety of sizes comes a variety of prices. Be prepared to spend more money for larger canners. All-American canners should only be used on a gas range instead of an electric one, so there is no stove damage. A feature of the All-American that makes them more user friendly is their weighted gauge. Instead of having to manually adjust the heat, weight on the valve regulates the pressure.

Presto pressure canners only come in two sizes which are the 16 quart liquid capacity model, and the 23 quart liquid capacity model. The Presto brand canners work with both gas and electric ranges. This fact, along with their small size, makes Presto more versatile than the All-American canners. The gauge is a dial gauge instead of a weighted one, and the pressure must be manually handled. This is better for people who wish to can in higher altitudes. Newer models have a button feature that drops down to inform you when the canner is safe to open.

As far as price goes, the Presto brand runs cheaper, and is more commonly available in stores such as Walmart. Presto canners do require the additional expense of replacing the rubber gasket around the inside of the lid. Gasket replacements are not very expensive however, and are only needed every few years. Keep in mind location when choosing between the two brands as well. High altitude places will prefer the presto while lower altitudes can enjoy the weighted gauge feature of the All-American.

The decision between the two is also dependent on batch sizes. Investing in a larger All-American pressure canner will be the smarter option for those who have a good amount of canning orders to do in a short time. Presto canners are better for casual canning. Both brands are well built and last a long time.

Just because All-American and Presto are the most well known brands on the market, does not mean they are the only brands. Mirro, while not as popular, is the only brand other than the two aforementioned brands that is most recognized by professionals in the field of canning. Mirro, like Presto, only comes in two sizes: Both of these sizes have weighted gauge features like All-American canners.

A pressure gauge is supposed to monitor and help regulate pressure inside of the canner. There are three different models of gauges that you can find on a pressure canner. The first and oldest is a dial gauge that is used to measure the pressure within the pot. The downside to this is that it can't control the pressure. A weighted gauge is the opposite: It controls the pressure but can't measure it. Lastly is a dual-gauge, which is a hybrid of the two. It has a dial for reading the pressure levels, but also utilizes weight to regulate that pressure.

A dial gauge pressure canner uses a dial to display the pressure that is present within the canner. As the temperature, as well as the pressure, builds up within the canner, the dial rises. Some gauges can show a half or a 1 pound increase in pressure while others are only marked for 5 pound increments. These pressure canners come in handy if you want to determine the pressure increments at higher altitudes. For instance, the pressure required for meats and vegetables is around 11 pounds if the altitude is less than 2000 feet. Unless you carefully monitor the gauge and adjust the heat, you cannot maintain the desired pressure within the pot. The gauges of these canners should be checked at least once a year to ensure their accuracy.

Similarly, a weighted gauge pressure canner uses a weight that regulates the pressure building up or present within the canner. These pressure canners have a single flat disc that has different markings for pressure such as 5 and 10. Some models of weighted gauge pressure canners have metal rings that can be stacked to regulate the pressure within the canner. For instance, if only 10 pounds of pressure is needed, two rings of 5 pounds each can be added. As the pressure starts building within the pot, the pressure causes the weight to jiggle. This is also an indicator the desired temperature is achieved within the pot. Some weights will jiggle a few times while others do it continuously. At altitudes of over 1,000 feet, don't forget to increase the pressure by 5 pounds.

The dual-gauge is just using both methods. Since weighted gauges are less hands on, the dial gauge is mostly there to keep track of where the pound per square inch or PSI is at. It can be a back up if something goes wrong, but to be honest, it is kind of useless. Modern Presto canners are mostly dial gauge, but they've made their pot compatible with dual-gauges. The weights are sold separately. This is helpful for people who prefer the dial gauge way, but aren't close enough to a local extension service to get their dial checked every year.

# Parts of a Pressure Canner

A pressure canner consists of several parts that are specially designed to help regulate the temperature as well as the steam pressure present within the canner. Understanding the different parts and the specific functions they perform will leave you better equipped to use your pressure canner. In this section, let's look at all the different parts of a pressure canner.

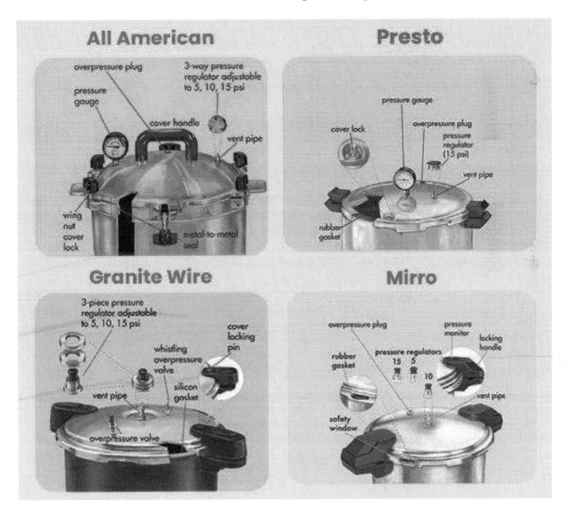

## *Pressure Regulator*

This part helps maintain and regulate the pressure within the canner. A peg usually holds the regulator in place. This feature ensures the pressure does not exceed 15 pounds within the canner.

## *Adjustable Pressure Regulator*

Some pressure canners have adjustable regulators to adjust the pressure within the pot. Such regulators give you the option to decide whether the pressure within the pot should be 5, 10, or 15 pounds. If the pressure regulator starts a gentle rhythmic rocking motion, it signals that the ideal pressure is maintained within the pot.

## *Vent Pipe*

The vent pipe is an important part of a pressure canner because it helps release excess pressure in the pot. It is a small opening where steam and pressure are vented out from the pot during the canning process. In some models, the vent pipe might be present on the lid itself. Ensure that you always check the vent pipe after every use because, at times, food or foam can clog it which prevents it from functioning effectively.

## *Air Vent*

The air vent is essentially a visual indicator of the pressure that's building up in the canner. Once sufficient pressure is present within the pot, the cover locks itself. This means opening it becomes impossible in any type of pressure canner. This is also a safety feature put in place to ensure the device is always closed under extreme pressure. The cover lock and air vent drop when the pressure inside the canner reduces.

## Locking Bracket

The locking bracket is present within the body of the pressure canner. This engages with the air vent to ensure the cover cannot be opened when pressure is present within the pot. All the pressure canners that were manufactured before 1978 do not have this feature.

## Sealing Ring

The sealing ring helps seal pressure within the body of the canner to ensure the pressure doesn't escape. It fits right around the pressure canner's cover and offers a tight pressure seal. It's present between the lid and the body of the pot. Sufficient pressure will not build within the canner if this ring is broken or not in place. It can handle the heat only from the pressure canner for as long as there are no tears or cracks in it.

## Pressure Dial Gauge

The dial gauge is a readable dial with a pointer that indicates the pressure present within the canner. You cannot use this to regulate the pressure. Instead, it is simply used to check the pressure within.

## Cooking Rack

The cooking rack is used for elevating food away from the liquid present in the pot. It also helps separate foods that you don't want to mix. You can use it for sterilizing as well. The cooking rack makes sure the jars or containers do not touch the bottom or the walls of the canner.

## Overpressure Plug

Another safety feature added is an overpressure plug. Any food clogging the vent pipes makes it difficult for the excess pressure to be let out of the body. In such instances, the steam will be automatically redirected from the overpressure plug. This plug usually pops out in case this happens. Heed it as a warning that you need to release the pressure from the part.

# Jars, Lids, and Other Canning Equipment

Canning at home is not only easy but is a rewarding activity, too. Whether it is delicious meat or vegetables, canning comes in handy. Once you have the required equipment, you simply need to follow the canning instructions given in the subsequent chapters. Here we will identify the equipment you need to can successfully.

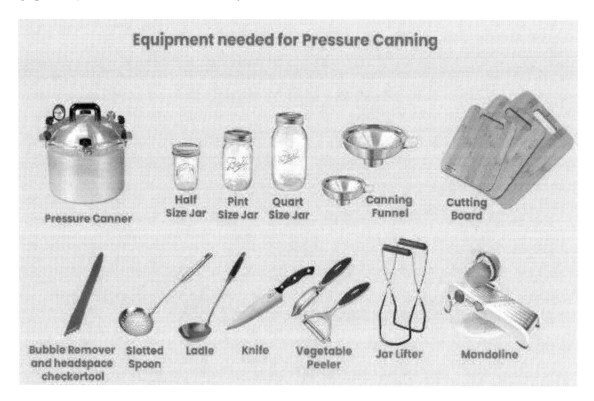

## Canning Jars and Lids

You cannot start canning without the required jars and lids. These days a variety of canning jars are available in different shapes as well as sizes. Depending on the items you want to can, the size of the jar will vary. These jars are good for repeated use provided you thoroughly clean and sterilize them. They are typically made of glass and can have a wide or regular mouth.

The lids of the canning jars have two parts—bands and lids. These are usually made of metal and fit the size of the jar's mouth. As long as the bands are in good shape, they can be reused but not the lids. You should never use the lids a second time; however, the bands can be used repeatedly.

## Utensils for Canning

Using a canning funnel makes things easier, especially to transfer liquids or semi-solid foods into the canning jars. Depending on the ingredients you are canning and the portions, the size of the funnel needed will vary.

You will also need a ladle for spooning the ingredients into the jars. Always opt for a stainless steel one because they are not only durable but are resistant to melting as well.

Once the jars are filled and you have put the lid on, it is time to put them in a pressure canner. This is where jar lifters come in handy. Using a jar lifter ensures you can do this process without accidentally dropping the jars or burning yourself. A jar lifter looks quite similar to a pair of metal tongs. The only difference is, they have a rubber coating on them and are ideal for lifting hot jars in and out of the pressure canner without any difficulty.

## A Canner

You need a pressure canner for pressure canning. In the previous section, you were introduced to different types of pressure canners and you can opt for one depending on your needs and requirements. Pressure canners can be used for almost all types of foods regardless of their acidity unlike water-bath canners. You will learn more about the differences between pressure and water-bath canners in the subsequent sections.

### *Kitchen Towels*

Regardless of what you are doing, you will need plenty of kitchen towels. This is a must-have for any kitchen project but is especially needed while canning. You can use them for setting hot jars on the counter and for cleaning the countertop too. A clean towel should be used for wiping the rim of the jar before you seal them. This prevents contamination. It also makes things look clean and tidy.

### *Food Strainer or Mill*

If you want to grind or puree foods for canning, you will need a food strainer or mill. These items also come in handy for other purposes and not just canning. Whether you are making homemade apple sauce or tomato puree, investing in one of these is a good idea.

# Water Bath vs. Pressure Canner

If you opt for the right canning method, the ingredients of your choice can be preserved safely and stored in your pantry for prolonged periods. However, this process becomes a little complicated if you are unsure of the method you are using. This is why it's important to understand the two different kinds of canning methods. The first one is known as water bath canning and the second is known as pressure canning. A boiling water-bath canner does not require any special equipment apart from the canning jars you need for storing food. On the other hand, pressure canning, as the name suggests, requires a pressure canner. Now that you know a pressure cooker is not the same as a canner let's learn the difference between water-bath canning and pressure canning.

If you want to opt for water-bath canning, you simply need a large pot that has a rack placed at the bottom. Whether it is a pot that's used for making soup or stock, any large pot can be used in this process. Fill the canning jars with the ingredients of your choice leaving the headspace recommended in the recipe and ensure the lids are secured tightly. Once the lids are in place, immerse these jars in boiling water for a specific time suggested by the canning recipe. Once you remove the jars from the boiling water of the water bath, let them cool down. In this process, a vacuum seal is formed between the jar and its lid. When it comes to using a water bath for canning, remember that the temperature of the water does not go beyond its boiling point.

On the other hand, a pressure canner is specifically designed for the purpose of pressure canning. It is a specialized piece of equipment that has various parts such as a pressure gauge, screw clamps, and a vent to ensure the pressure within the canner is not restricted to the temperature of boiling water. So, when the jars filled with food are placed in it, they are heated beyond the boiling point of water. A wonderful thing about a pressure canner is regardless of the pH of the food, you can pretty much can anything you want. If you are trying to can foods that are alkaline or low in acid, opt for a pressure canner. Even though botulism-causing bacteria cannot survive the temperature of boiling water (212°F), the spores can. Unless the temperature is greater than 212°F, the risk of botulism cannot be eliminated. This is where a pressure canner steps into the picture. You will learn more about how a pressure canner neutralizes the risk of botulism in the next sections.

## Important Considerations While Canning

If you have a canner and other equipment, canning at home is easy. That said, certain external factors are also responsible for the longevity of the food you canned. Three important factors that home canning enthusiasts must pay attention to are altitude, temperature, and acidity. These three factors make all the difference between a successful attempt and a poorly canned jar of food.

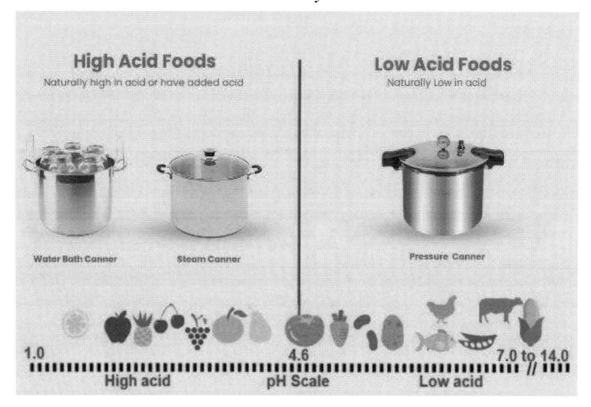

To determine how acidic or alkaline things are, a scientific measure known as the pH scale is used. The markings on this scale extend between 0 to 14. If the pH is between 0-6, it is known to be acidic, with 7 being neutral and above that is what is known as basic or alkaline pH. The stronger the acidic pH, the closer to 0. Are you wondering what this has to do with canning? An important benefit of pressure canning is it helps eliminate botulism-causing spores and bacteria. Acidity plays a vital role here. Common foods that are low in acidity score are milk, fresh vegetables, red meats, seafood, and poultry. Their pH is above 4.6. Any other ingredient with such a weakly acidic pH must be sterilized at temperatures between 240-250°F to ensure the harmful spores are killed. This is perfectly attainable while using pressure canners. The only exception to this is tomatoes because of their high acidity. Other high-acid foods such as jams, pickles, fruits, jellies, and such usually have a pH lower than 4.6. These can be canned using a regular water bath canner.

## *Temperature*

The boiling point of water is 212°F. Regardless of the time spent boiling the water, it will not exceed this temperature. After the water reaches its boiling point, evaporation starts. This is a primary reason why water-bath canning is not the best method for preserving and canning low-acid foods. When water is heated up in a closed container, the temperature increases. This is due to the added pressure in the form of evaporating water. Due to this simple mechanism at play, pressure canning is ideal for any type of food. While using a pressure canner, there is an additional 10-11 pounds of pressure that increases the water beyond its boiling point and brings it up to 240°F. This is the temperature desired for destroying botulism-causing bacteria and their spores. It effectively halts their germination cycle by destroying all their traces from the food within the jars.

Certain factors reduce the temperature present within the pressure canner. One such thing is an inaccurate dial reading or low temperature of the air present within the canner. This is one of the reasons why the canner must be allowed to vent for at least 10 minutes. This helps expel the cold air present within. Before you place the weight or the pressure regulator, ensure that you let the pressure canner vent for a while. If the pressure canner has dial gauges, then make sure you check the gauges annually to maintain their accuracy.

# *Altitude*

| Altitude in Feet | Weighted Gauge in Pounds | Dial Gauge in Pounds | Weighted Gauge in Kilopascal | Dial Gauge in Kilopascal |
|---|---|---|---|---|
| 0-1,000 (0-304 m) | 10 | 11 | 69 | 76 |
| 1,001 - 2,000 (305-609 m) | 15 | 11 | 103 | 76 |
| 2,001 - 4,000 (610-1,219 m) | 15 | 12 | 103 | 83 |
| 4,001-6000 (1,220-1,828 m) | 15 | 13 | 103 | 90 |
| 6,001 -8,000 (1,829 -2,483 m) | 15 | 14 | 103 | 97 |
| 8,001 - 10,000 (2,439 - 3,048m) | 15 | 15 | 103 | 103 |

This table shows the pressure required at various altitudes to reach 240°F (115° C) inside the pressure canner. Once the correct pressure for these altitudes is applied, the processing time is the same at all altitudes.

The next important external factor that you must pay attention to while home canning is the altitude. It's repeatedly mentioned that the boiling point of water is 212°F. However, did you know that this is the boiling point of water at sea level? When the altitude increases water can boil at a lower temperature. This is why you need to pay attention to altitude while canning. The time or temperature has to be changed accordingly depending on the altitude to ensure harmful pathogens are not present in the jars you are canning.

As the altitude increases the time taken for canning along with the temperature to be maintained during this process will increase. While using a pressure canner, the time taken for canning prescribed by most recipes will stay the same. That said, the pounds of pressure that need to be applied have to be increased. If you are using a weighted gauge pressure canner and are at an altitude of over 1000 feet, then food is normally sterilized at 15 pounds pressure. If the altitude is between 1,000-2,000 feet, 11 pounds of pressure is sufficient to attain the same results. However, the pressure must be increased to 12 pounds if the altitude is between 2,000-4,000 feet. Similarly, for an altitude of 4,000-6,000 feet, the pressure needed is 13 pounds whereas it is 14 pounds when the altitude is between 6,000-8,000 feet.

Learning about this is needed because the cooking time is crucial to ensure the ingredients are properly sterilized and processed. Depending on the altitude of the area you reside in, the recipes given in this book must be adjusted.

## *Risk of Botulism*

Botulism is a type of food poisoning that's caused by a specific strain of bacteria known as *Clostridium botulinum*. Spores of this specific bacteria are commonly present on all food surfaces. Chances are you have heard of the risk of botulism in canned foods. It usually occurs upon the consumption of improperly canned food. It probably makes canned food seem risky but with a few safe practices, you can eliminate this health hazard.

If the spores of this bacteria are present on all surfaces, then shouldn't eating any food be harmful? Well, the thing is, these spores are harmless when present on the surface of fresh foods. Understand that there is a difference between harmless spores and a full-blown infestation of the bacteria. Under the right conditions, these spores germinate, multiply, and diet. This cycle keeps repeating until they have fully contaminated the food. As these bacteria multiply and die, they release a toxic compound causing botulism. This renders the food unfit for consumption.

The absence of oxygen and low temperature are the two external factors the spores of botulism-causing bacteria need to develop. The ideal temperature for their germination is between 70-120°F. Canned foods meet both these basic needs. Therefore, you need to be extra careful while canning foods, especially ones with low acidity. When food is canned using a pressure canner, the pressure within the canner helps increase the temperature of water beyond its boiling point. The temperature within it can be up to 240° F, which is sufficient to destroy the spores of this harmful bacteria.

# Things to Remember

Here are some simple points you must remember while using a pressure canner:

- If you are using a dial gauge pressure canner, ensure the gauge is checked for accuracy. You should do it once a year. Ideally, get the dial inspected right before the canning season.

- If you are using a weighted gauge pressure canner, the units of pressure exerted by it are 5, 10, and 15 pounds. Depending on the altitude, the pressure required will vary. For instance, if you need 12 pounds of pressure, opt for the next closest weight, which is a 15-pound weight.

- One important thing that you must not forget while using pressure canners is to always check the vent openings after and before every use. A visual check helps ensure nothing is obstructing the vent. You can also run a string through the opening. If the vent is clogged the pressure within the canner will become too high. This, in turn, means the overpressure plug can blow. To ensure there isn't an accidental explosion while using a pressure canner, check the vents.

- As the altitude increases pay extra attention to the pressure within the canner. At higher altitudes, the pressure within the canner is lower, and therefore the temperature is lower too. Whenever you are using a canner at a higher altitude, increase and adjust the pressure accordingly.

- If there is any air trapped within the canner during the process the temperature reduces. This, in turn, increases the risk of under-processing. The simplest way to avoid this is by allowing the pressure canner to vent for 10 minutes.

# Chapter 2:

# How to Pressure Can

*"To eat is a necessity, but to eat intelligently is an art."*

François de la Rochefoucauld

Learning about pressure canning and how your pressure canner works is the first step toward becoming a successful home canner. Now, it is time to get to the interesting part of canning — learning about the process involved.

# Basic Steps of Pressure Canning

Now that you have all the required equipment and tools, it is time to start pressure canning. It might sound intimidating, especially if you are trying it for the first time, but it is not. Once you go through the steps discussed in this section, you can become a pro in no time.

## *Step 1: Heating the Jars*

This step helps sterilize the jars before they are ready for canning. Place the empty jars without their lids in the canner. Do not place the lid on the canner. Pour hot water into the canner such that the jars are completely immersed in it and the water is about an inch above the jars. Ensure you use hot water and not boiling water. Turn on the heat and let the water come to a boil over high heat. Once the water comes to a rolling boil within the canner, turn off the heat after 10 minutes. Carefully remove the jars from the canner and set them out on a clean surface to dry. Ensure you use tongs or a lifter for removing the jars, because they can be quite hot. Wipe the jars thoroughly with a clean cloth.

## *Step 2: Filling the Jars*

Once the jars are sterilized, it is time to fill them! ensure they are still warm at this stage. Never fill jars when they are cold because it increases the risk of contamination. While filling the jars, ensure you leave about an inch of headspace between the food and lid to create a vacuum seal. Don't tightly pack the jars because this can cause the food to expand and bubble out during the canning process.

### Step 3: Remove any Air Bubbles

Now, chances are there will be some air bubbles within the jar. You might not even see them at times. Use a thin and flexible spatula, to remove air bubbles. To do this, simply slip in the spatula and move it around to release any trapped air. If there is any more space, you can top it up again.

### Step 4: Add the Lids

Once you have filled the jars, don't forget to wipe their rims. Do this before adding the lid. Set the lid in place and screw it tight. This is crucial to ensure that air does not enter the jar.

### Step 5: Lock the Pressure Canner Lid

As and when you start filling the jars, place them in the pressure canner. While doing this, there should be sufficient water in the canner so that only a few inches of them are covered. Ensure the jars are not submerged. Set the lid of the canner in place and twist so the handles lock.

## Step 6: Venting

Now, it is time to turn on the heat and let steam start building up in the pressure canner. You will see a full head of steam blowing out of the vent. Let it go on for 10 minutes before adding the regulator on top of the steam spout.

## Step 7: The Right Pressure

If you have a weighted gauge regulator, make sure it is set at the right weight. The weight you should use will usually be specified in your recipe. Keep in mind, different altitudes have different requirements for the amount of weight you should put on it. Oftentimes, it is anywhere between 10 to 15 pounds of pressure. If you don't have a weighted gauge model just pay attention to your dial gauge. Be careful when you place the regulator on the steam spout as it can be very hot: Oven mitts will keep you safe from the heat.

You need to let the pressure canner reach the required pressure for canning. If it has a safety valve, it will pop up showing that sufficient pressure is there within. If for any reason your pressure goes below the recommended amount, you need to bring the pressure back up and start the timer over again.

Never open the lid of the pressure canner if its regulator starts rocking. The pot is full of boiling hot steam that can burn you or anyone else nearby. Adjust the heat so it starts making a constant rattling sound. If the recipe has a specific time, adjust it accordingly.

## Step 8: Depressurize

Once the time prescribed by the recipe is up, it is time to turn off the heat. Do not make the mistake of opening the lid right away. Ensure the safety valves are back in their place before attempting to open the lid. Even if you feel a slight resistance, give it a while longer to fully depressurize. Remove the regulator and then open the lid such that the steam isn't directed at you.

## Step 9: Cool the Jars

Using a kitchen towel or jar lifter, carefully lift the jars out of the pressure canner. Usually, letting them stay in the pot for up to ten minutes ensures they are relatively cool before removing them. Do not try tightening the lids at this stage. Set the jars on a kitchen towel or a wire rack to let them cool down. Usually, it is recommended to leave the jars undisturbed for 12-24 hours. Do not try to tighten the bands on the jar lids or push down on the flat lid until the jar is fully cooled. If any jars seem improperly sealed, refrigerate them immediately if not consumed right away.

After all this, do not forget to spend some time cleaning the pressure canner, cleaning the canner's pot, the gasket, and the lid. Remove the safety valves and clean, wash, and dry them too.

Once you complete these nine steps, you have successfully completed canning your first batch at home! Yes, it is as easy as that! You simply need to pay attention to the temperature, pressure, and time limits prescribed by the recipe of your choice!

Date the lid of the jars with a permanent marker so you can know when they go bad. The lid will be discarded later, so you don't need to mark the jar's glass every time. It will also be helpful to label the jar with its ingredients just in case you forget later on. Most people store their canned goods in their basement but it doesn't matter where you put them as long as it is cool and dry. It is also important that it is out of direct sunlight as that can spoil the food faster. For optimal quality, canned goods should be used within one year.

## Essential Practices

When it comes to canning, there is a learning curve. It takes consistency, effort, and practice to get the hang of canning techniques. If you want stellar results while canning, be careful while following the different steps involved in the process. You will also be introduced to different tips and suggestions that can be used to improve the quality or chances of success you achieve while canning.

Before you decide to start canning, it's important to test the pressure canner. Whether you are testing the accuracy, the sealing ring, or the pressure that can develop, check everything. Once you know the appliance is working as intended, obtaining better results while canning becomes probable.

If you want to get good results, you must follow the recipe and USDA guidelines carefully. There's room for experimentation. That said, always learn the basics fast. It's also important to focus on the basics and USDA guidelines because food safety is crucial.

Ensure that you are handling the jars with care. When removing them from the pressure canner, use a jar lifter. Ensure the jars are always placed in an upright position. Another thing that you must check for is to ensure the jars are sealed properly.

Whenever you are canning, make sure that you are using sufficient water. Water starts evaporating from the pot in the form of steam. Water is the barrier between the jars and the bottom of the pot. If there is no water, the jars will be in direct contact with high heat.

Canning is a simple process, but it is usually quite messy. To reduce the mess, use aluminum foil to cover the work surface. Even cover the countertop with one or two layouts of aluminum foil. Once done, you simply need to wad the foil up and throw it in the bin.

The role played by heat and pressure cannot be ignored when it comes to pressure canning. Depending on the altitude, the temperature needs to be adjusted. Go through the information given in the previous section about pressure, altitude, and acidity while canning. Another important aspect you must remember when it comes to temperature is to ensure the jars are warm when you fill them up. Also, don't forget to immediately place the jars in the canner as soon as they are filled.

Before you decide to open the lid of the pressure canner, ensure the pressure has dissipated. It simply means turning off with heat and waiting for a couple of minutes until the pressure reduces. If you notice even a little resistance while trying to open the lid, let it cool down for a while longer.

Make sure everything is thoroughly cleaned before getting started. It means, you must not only clean the jars and lids but the canner and the countertops too. Ensure all items and surfaces you come in contact with while canning is clean. This reduces the risk of cross-contamination.

# Chapter 3:
# Lentils and Beans

## Dried Beans

Makes: 7 pint jars (500 ml) or 14 ½ pint jars (250 ml)

**Ingredients:**

- 2 pounds (907 g) dried beans like pinto beans, black-eyed peas, black beans, peas, kidney beans, etc.

- Boiling water, as required

- ¼ teaspoon (1.4 g) salt per half pint jar or ½ teaspoon (2.8 g) salt per pint size jar (optional)

**Directions:**

1. To start off, pick the beans for any dirt, stones, discolored beans etc. Rinse the beans with fresh water and soak in a large pot of water. Soak them for at least 12 hours. Discard the soaked water.

2. If you do not want to soak the beans for 12 hours, there is another way you can do it: Place beans in a saucepan and cover with water. The water should be at least 2 to 3 inches over the beans. Place the saucepan over high heat and wait for it to start boiling. Let it boil for two minutes and turn off the heat. Let the beans soak in the hot water for an hour.

3. Transfer the beans into a large stock pot. Cover the beans with fresh water and place the stock pot over high heat. When water begins to boil, lower the heat slightly and cook for about 30 minutes or until the beans are tender.

4. Now the next thing to do is to arrange the pressure canner, canning lids and jars. You need seven 1 pint jars (500 ml) or fourteen ½ pint jars (250 ml).

5. Pour enough water into the pressure canner following the manufacturer's instructions such that it is about 3 inches (8 cm) in height from the bottom of the canner. Place the canner on your stovetop over low heat. Place the jars in the canner so that the jars remain warm. The temperature of the water in the canner should be maintained at 180°F (82°C). Place the lids in a small saucepan of water over low heat on another burner.

6. Boil a kettle of water. Lift the jars from the canner and place over the towel. Sprinkle salt in each jar if using.

7. Carefully ladle the beans into the jars along with the cooked liquid. Make sure the beans are equally distributed among the jars. If the beans are not covered in water, pour enough boiling water to cover the beans to get headspace of 1 inch (2.5 cm) and make sure to remove bubbles using a bubble removing tool. Reassess the headspace and pour more water if required.

8. Take a clean damp cloth and wipe the rim of the jars. Place the canning lid on each jar using the lid lifter. Place the canning ring on each jar and tighten it as suggested.

9. Place the jars in the canner and process the jars following the manufacturer's instruction manual at 10 psi (69 kPa). Set the timer for 75 minutes adjusting for altitude if required. Once the timer goes off, turn off the burner.

10. Once you are done with the processing, let the pressure release naturally before opening the canner and taking out the jars. Let the jars cool completely on your countertop for no less than 12 hours. Wipe the jars with a dry kitchen cloth or paper towel. Make sure to check for the seals. Use the beans within a year.

11. **Serving suggestion**: You can use these beans to serve with meat or add it into soups or salads. Warm them up before serving.

# Lentils with Vegetables

Makes: 4 pint jars (500 ml)

**Ingredients:**

- 1 ½ pounds (680 g) dried lentils

- 1-2 fresh celery stalks

- Five cloves garlic

- One large onion

- A large handful chopped greens like kale, Swiss chard, green cabbage or any other greens of your choice

- Two basil leaves, minced

- ¼ teaspoon (14 g) dried oregano

- 3 cups (710 ml) low-fat, low-sodium organic beef broth

- ¼ teaspoon ground black pepper

- 1/8 teaspoon (0.4 g) red pepper flakes or to taste

- ½ tablespoon (7.2 g) salt

Serving instructions per 1 pint jar (500 ml):

1. Grated parmesan cheese to garnish

2. Salt and pepper to taste

3. Any seasoning to taste (optional)

4. Chopped parsley to garnish

5. Some cooked noodles or browned ground beef crumbles (optional)

6. Squeeze of lemon or lime juice (optional)

**Directions:**

1. Place lentils in a large pot and cover with enough water such that the water is about 2 to 3 inches over the lentils. Let the lentils soak overnight. If you are short of time and are not able to soak them overnight, then place the pot over high heat and wait for the water to start boiling. Once the water starts boiling, let the lentils cook for two minutes. Turn off the heat and let them soak for an hour.

2. The following morning (after soaking the lentils overnight), have your other ingredients ready. Finely chop the celery stalks, garlic, and onion. Check the greens for any wild plants and discard them. Rinse the greens well and discard the stems. Chop the leaves into smaller pieces if desired.

3. Now the next thing to do is to arrange the pressure canner, canning lids and jars. You need four 1 pint jars (500 ml).

4. Pour enough water into the pressure canner following the manufacturer's instructions such that it is about 3 inches (8 cm) in height from the bottom of the canner. Place the canner on your stovetop over low heat. Place the jars in the canner so that the jars remain warm. The temperature of the water in the canner should be maintained at 180°F (82°C). Place the lids in a small saucepan of water over low heat on another burner.

5. Now add celery, garlic, onion, greens, herbs, broth, salt, and spices into a stock pot and place the pot over high heat on your stovetop. When the mixture starts boiling, lower the heat and cook for 15 minutes. Turn off the heat.

6. Lift the jars from the canner with a jar lifting tongs and place over the towel. Place funnel over the rim of the jars and carefully add lentils and vegetables into the jars using the slotted spoon. Fill the lentils up to 2/3 of the jars. Make sure the lentils and vegetables are equally distributed among the jars.

7. Now pour the hot stock into the jars until you get a headspace of 1 inch (2.5 cm). If the stock is not sufficient, boil some hot water in a kettle and pour into the jars. Make sure

to remove bubbles using a bubble removing tool. Reassess the headspace and pour more boiling water or hot stock if required.

8. Take a clean damp cloth and wipe the rim of the jars. Place the canning lid on each jar using the lid lifter. Place the canning ring on each jar and tighten it as suggested.

9. Place the jars in the canner and process the jars following the manufacturer's instruction manual at 10 psi (69 kPa). Set the timer for 75 minutes adjusting for altitude if required. Once the timer goes off, turn off the burner.

10. Once you are done with the processing, let the pressure release naturally before opening the canner and taking out the jars. Let the jars cool completely on your countertop for no less than 12 hours. Wipe the jars with a dry kitchen cloth or paper towel. Make sure to check for the seals. Use the lentils within a year.

11. **Serving suggestion**: Empty the contents of a jar into a saucepan. Heat the lentils over medium heat on your stovetop. Add cooked noodles or beef if desired. Add salt and pepper to taste. If you like to dilute the lentils, add some water or stock while heating the lentils. Ladle into bowls. Garnish with parsley and parmesan cheese and serve.

# Baked Beans

Makes: 6 pint jars (500 ml)

**Ingredients:**

- 2.2 pounds (1 kg) dried navy beans

- 12 ounces (340 g) tomato paste

- 3 teaspoons (15 g) mustard powder

- 3 teaspoons (15 g) ground black pepper

- 2 tablespoons (30 g) kitchen bouquet (optional)

- 6 cups (1.5 L) cooked bean water

- Two medium onions, chopped

- 3 tablespoons (30 g) Worcestershire sauce

- 3 teaspoons (15 g) salt

- 6 tablespoons (90 g) brown sugar

- Four bay leaves

Serving instructions per 1 pint jar (500 ml):

- Sweet chili sauce to taste

- Chopped cooked sausages

- Salad or cooked pasta

## Directions:

1. Place beans in a stock pot and cover with water. The water should be at least 2 to 3 inches (5 to 7.5 cm) over the beans. Place the pot over high heat and wait for it to start boiling. Let it boil for two minutes and turn off the heat. Let the beans soak in the hot water for an hour. Make sure to cover the pot while the beans are soaking.

2. Meanwhile combine onions, Worcestershire sauce, salt, brown sugar, tomato paste, mustard, pepper, and kitchen bouquet in a large microwave safe bowl. Keep it aside as of now.

3. Drain off the water and put the beans in a large pot. Add bay leaves and cover with water. The water should be at least 2 to 3 inches (5 to 7.5 cm) over the beans. Place the pot over high heat and wait for it to start boiling. Let it boil for 1-2 minutes and turn off the heat. Do not boil the beans longer than two minutes or else you will end up with mashed beans.

4. You also need to arrange the pressure canner, canning lids and jars. You need six 1 pint jars (500 ml). Pour enough water into the pressure canner following the manufacturer's

instructions such that it is about 3 inches (8 centimeters) in height from the bottom of the canner. Place the canner on your stovetop over low heat. Place the jars in the canner so that the jars remain warm. The temperature of the water in the canner should be maintained at 180°F (82°C). Place the lids in a small saucepan of water over low heat on another burner.

5.  Now place a colander over a large bowl and drain the beans into the colander. Do not discard the cooked liquid. You need some of it to make the sauce. The bay leaves are no longer needed.

6.  Pour 6 cups (1.5 L) of the drained liquid into the microwave safe bowl with the sauce ingredients and stir. Cover the bowl and place it in the microwave. Cook on high power for about seven minutes. Or until you get a nice sauce. Take out the bowl and stir the sauce.

7.  Distribute the beans among the jars. You should be able to fill each jar up to about ¾ the jar. Pour the sauce mixture into the jars until you get a headspace of 1 inch (2.5 cm). It is better to use a funnel while pouring sauce into the jars.

8.  Make sure to remove bubbles using a bubble removing tool. Reassess the headspace and add more of the mixture into the jar.

9.  Take a clean damp cloth and wipe the rim of the jars. Place the canning lid on each jar using the lid lifter. Place the canning ring on each jar and tighten it as suggested.

10. Place the jars in the canner and process the jars following the manufacturer's instruction manual at 10 psi (69 kPa). Set the timer for 65 minutes adjusting for altitude if required. Once the timer goes off, turn off the burner.

11. Once you are done with the processing, let the pressure release naturally before opening the canner and taking out the jars. Let the jars cool completely on your countertop for no less than 12 hours. Wipe the jars with a dry kitchen cloth or paper towel. Make sure to check for the seals. These jars will last you for 12 to 15 months.

12. **Serving suggestion**: There are numerous ways of serving baked beans. You can serve it over toasted bread. You can serve eggs over beans. You can serve it as a side dish along

with meat. You can mash up the beans and serve as a bean mash. You can also make muffins or frittatas using the baked beans.

Here is one favorite way I use the baked beans: Empty the contents of a baked beans can into a saucepan. Add sweet chili sauce and sausages and heat it over medium heat until very nice and hot. Serve it over hot cooked pasta or along with a salad.

# Chili Con Carne

Makes: 11 pint jars (500 ml)

**Ingredients:**

- 1 ½ pounds (680 g) dried kidney beans

- 1 ½ pounds (680 g) lean ground beef

- Three cloves garlic, minced

- 1 ½ tablespoons (22 ml) oil

- 1 ½ large onions, chopped

- 3 tablespoons (42 g) chili powder

- 1 tablespoon (15 g) salt

- 1 ½ tablespoons (21 g) beef bouillon granules powder

- ½ tablespoon (7.5 g) onion powder

- 1 ½ cans {14.5 ounces (400 g) each} diced tomatoes

- 1 ½ cups (350 ml) water

- ½ tablespoon (7.5 g) sugar

- 1 tablespoon (15 g) ground cumin

- ½ teaspoon (2.8 g) freshly ground black pepper

- ½ teaspoon (2.8 g) garlic powder

- ½ can {from a 14.5 ounces (400 g) can} tomato sauce

Serving instructions per 1 pint jar (500 ml):
- Salt and pepper to taste

- Chopped parsley to garnish

**Directions:**

1. To start off, pick the beans for any dirt, stones, discolored beans etc. Rinse the beans with fresh water and soak in a large pot of water. Soak them for at least 12 hours. Discard the soaked water.

2. If you do not want to soak the beans for 12 hours, there is another way you can do it: Place beans in a saucepan and cover with water. The water should be at least 2 to 3 inches over the beans. Place the saucepan over high heat and wait for it to start boiling. Let it boil for two minutes and turn off the heat. Let the beans soak in the hot water for an hour. Drain off the water.

3. Transfer the beans into a large stock pot. Cover the beans with fresh water and place the stock pot over high heat. When water begins to boil, lower the heat slightly (i.e. medium heat) and cook for about 30 minutes or until the beans are tender. Turn off the heat and drain off the liquid. Rinse the beans well and put it aside for the time being.

4. Now the next thing to do is to arrange the pressure canner, canning lids and jars. You need eleven 1 pint jars (500 ml).

5. Pour enough water into the pressure canner following the manufacturer's instructions such that it is about 3 inches (8 centimeters) in height from the bottom of the canner. Place the canner on your stovetop over low heat. Place the jars in the canner so that the jars remain warm. The temperature of the water in the canner should be maintained at 180°F (82°C). Place the lids in a small saucepan of water over low heat on another burner.

6. While the canner is slowly heating, pour oil into a large stock pot and let the oil heat over high heat. Once the oil is hot, add ground beef and cook until brown. As you stir, break the beef into crumbles. Stir in the onions and garlic and cook until the onions turn tender. This should take around 7-8 minutes. Discard as much fat as you can from the pot.

7. Now add pepper, onion powder, garlic powder, cumin, beef bouillon powder, and chili powder, and keep stirring for about a minute or until you get a nice aroma. Add beans, tomato sauce, diced tomatoes, salt, and sugar and mix well. When the mixture starts boiling, bring down the heat to low heat and let the mixture cook for about 3-4 minutes. Make sure to stir often. Turn off the heat.

8. Lift the jars from the canner with a jar lifting tongs and place over the towel. Place funnel over the rim of the jars and carefully spoon the mixture into the jars until you get headspace of 1 inch (2.5 cm). It is better to use a funnel while spooning into the jars.

9. Make sure to remove bubbles using a bubble removing tool. Reassess the headspace and add more of the mixture into the jar.

10. Take a clean damp cloth and wipe the rim of the jars. Place the canning lid on each jar using the lid lifter. Place the canning ring on each jar and tighten it as suggested.

11. Place the jars in the canner and process the jars following the manufacturer's instruction manual at 10 psi (69 kPa). Set the timer for 75 minutes adjusting for altitude if required. Once the timer goes off, turn off the burner.

12. Once you are done with the processing, let the pressure release naturally before opening the canner and taking out the jars. Let the jars cool completely on your countertop for no less than 12 hours. Wipe the jars with a dry kitchen cloth or paper towel. Make sure to check for the seals. These jars will last you for 12 to 15 months.

13. **Serving suggestion**: Empty the contents of a jar into a saucepan. Heat the chili over medium heat on your stovetop. Ladle into bowls. Add some salt and pepper to taste if desired. Garnish with parsley or any other fresh herbs of your choice and serve.

# Pork and Beans

Makes: 6 pint jars (500 ml) or 3 quart jars (1 L)

**Ingredients:**

- 1 ½ pounds (680 g) dried navy beans or white beans

- 2 tablespoons (30 ml) apple cider vinegar

- 1 tablespoon (15 g) ground dry mustard

- 2-3 tablespoons (30–45 g) brown sugar or to taste

- 1 tablespoon (15 ml) Worcestershire sauce

- ¾ pound (340 g) bacon, diced

- Three cloves garlic, peeled, minced

- 2-3 tablespoons (30–45 ml) molasses (optional)

- 1 ½ tablespoons (22.5 g) kosher salt

- ¼ cup (120 ml) ketchup

- Two medium onions, chopped

- ½ teaspoon (2.5 g) ground black pepper

- Two bay leaves

- ¼ teaspoon (1.25 g) ground cloves

Serving instructions per 1 pint jar (500 ml):

- Grated parmesan cheese

- Chopped fresh herbs of your choice

**Directions:**

1. Place beans in a stock pot and cover with water. The water should be at least 2 to 3 inches (5 to 7.5 cm) over the beans. Place the pot over high heat and wait for it to start boiling. Let it boil for two minutes and turn off the heat. Let the beans soak in the hot water for an hour. Make sure to cover the pot while the beans are soaking.

2. Drain off the water and put the beans in a large stock pot. Pour 3.5 quarts (4.5 L) into the pot. Place the pot over high heat and wait for it to start boiling. Let it boil for two minutes and turn off the heat.

3. Now place a colander over a large bowl and drain the beans into the colander. Do not discard the cooked liquid.

4. Now put the bacon into a large stock pot and cook over medium heat on your stovetop until bacon turns crisp. Discard all the cooked fat from the pot. Next, put the onions into the pot and stir-fry for a few minutes until the onions turn pink. Stir in the garlic and cook for about a minute or until you get a nice aroma. Add beans, vinegar, mustard, brown sugar, Worcestershire sauce, molasses if using, salt, ketchup, pepper, bay leaves, and ground cloves.

5. Pour the drained liquid into the stock pot and stir the ingredients until well combined. When the mixture starts boiling, lower the heat and cook covered, until the beans are slightly tender. Make sure the beans are not overcooked as they have to be processed in the canner as well. If you find the liquid less in the pot at any time, feel free to add more

6. You also need to arrange the pressure canner, canning lids and jars. You can do this after about 30 minutes after you start cooking the beans. You need seven 1 pint jars (500 ml) or three quart size (1 L) jars. Pour enough water into the pressure canner following the manufacturer's instructions such that it is about 3 inches (8 centimeters) in height from the bottom of the canner. Place the canner on your stovetop over low heat. Place the jars in the canner so that the jars remain warm. The temperature of the water in the canner should be maintained at 180°F (82°C). Place the lids in a small saucepan of water over low heat on another burner.

7. Place the jars over a towel on your countertop. It is better to use a funnel while pouring the beans into the jars. Remove beans with a slotted spoon and place them in the jars. Make sure to distribute the beans equally among the jars. Pour enough cooked liquid from the pot into the jars until you get headspace of 1 inch (2.5 cm).

8. Make sure to remove bubbles using a bubble removing tool. Reassess the headspace and add more of the liquid into jars if required. In case you run short of liquid, you can compensate by pouring boiling water to fill up to the required headspace.

9. Take a clean damp cloth and wipe the rim of the jars. Place the canning lid on each jar using the lid lifter. Place the canning ring on each jar and tighten it as suggested.

10. Place the jars in the canner and process the jars following the manufacturer's instruction manual at 10 psi (69 kPa). Set the timer for 65 minutes if you are using pint size jars or 75 minutes if you are using quart size jars, adjusting for altitude if required. Once the timer goes off, turn off the burner.

11. Once you are done with the processing, let the pressure release naturally before opening the canner and taking out the jars. Let the jars cool completely on your countertop for no less than 12 hours. Wipe the jars with a dry kitchen cloth or paper towel. Make sure to check for the seals. These jars will last you for about 12 months.

12. **Serving suggestion**: Empty the contents of a jar into a saucepan. Heat over medium heat on your stovetop. Ladle into bowls. Add some salt and pepper to taste if desired. Garnish with cheese and any other fresh herbs of your choice and serve.

# Chapter 4:

# Tomatoes

## Canning Tomatoes

Makes: 4 pint jars (500 ml) or 2 quart jars (1 L)

### Ingredients:

- 6 pounds (2.7 kg) fresh, ripe plum tomatoes

- Boiling water, as required

- ½ teaspoon salt per pint size jar or 1 teaspoon salt per quart size jar (optional)

### Use any one of these acidic ingredients: (This is important)

- 1 tablespoon lemon juice per pint size jar or 2 tablespoons lemon juice per quart size jar (preferably bottled lemon juice)

- 2 tablespoons 5% acidic vinegar per pint size jar or 4 tablespoons 5% acidic vinegar per quart size jar

- ¼ teaspoon citric acid per pint size jar or ½ teaspoon citric acid per quart size jar

### Directions:

1. Boil a pot of water over high heat. While the water is boiling, rinse the tomatoes well. Remove any stem or leaves from the tomatoes. Make an 'X' on the top of each tomato using a paring knife.

2. Have a bowl of ice water ready on your countertop near the stovetop. Drop the tomatoes carefully into the pot with boiling water. Let the tomatoes cook for a minute. Soon you can see a bit of loose skin around the area of the 'X' on the tomatoes.

3. Pick the tomatoes with a slotted spoon and drop them into the bowl of ice water. In a few minutes the tomatoes would have cooled down. Peel off the skin from the tomatoes.

4. Put the peeled tomatoes into a large bowl.

5. While you are peeling the tomatoes, arrange the pressure canner, canning lids, and jars. You need two quart (1 L) size jars or four 1 pint jars (500 ml). Pour enough water into the pressure canner following the manufacturer's instructions such that it is about 3 inches (8 centimeters) in height from the bottom of the canner. Place the canner on your stovetop over low heat. Place the jars in the canner so that the jars remain warm. The temperature of the water in the canner should be maintained at 180°F (82°C). Place the lids in a small saucepan of water over low heat on another burner.

6. Place a kitchen towel on your countertop and spread it. Lift the jars from the canner and place over the towel. Add the chosen acidic ingredient in each jar. Add the salt if using. Place the tomatoes in the jars until you get a headspace of ¼ inch (1.25 cm). It is better to use a funnel while adding the sauce into the jars.

7. Make sure to remove bubbles using a bubble removing tool. Reassess the headspace. On reassessing, if the headspace increases, pour some liquid of the tomatoes that has been collected in the bowl. If there is no liquid in the tomatoes, add some boiling water.

8. Take a clean damp cloth and wipe the rim of the jars. Place the canning lid on each jar using the lid lifter. Place the canning ring on each jar and tighten it as suggested.

9. Place the jars in the canner and process the jars following the manufacturer's instruction manual at 10 psi (69 kPa). Set the timer for 65 minutes adjusting for altitude if required. Once the timer goes off, turn off the burner.

10. Once you are done with the processing, let the pressure release naturally before opening the canner and taking out the jars. Let the jars cool completely on your countertop for no less than 12 hours. Wipe the jars with a dry kitchen cloth or paper towel. Make sure to check for the seals. These jars will last you for 12 to 15 months.

11. **Serving suggestion**: You can use tomatoes in just almost anything like curries, sauces, etc. Use as much as required and store the remaining in the refrigerator.

# Spaghetti Sauce

Makes: 4 pints

**Ingredients:**

- 15 pounds (6.8 kg) Roma tomatoes or any fresh tomatoes

- 1 large onion, chopped

- 1 tablespoon salt

- 2 – 3 cloves garlic, peeled, minced

- ½ pound (227 g) mushrooms, sliced (optional)

- 1 tablespoon dried oregano flakes

- 2 tablespoons (25 g) brown sugar or unrefined cane sugar

- 2 tablespoons (28.4 g) butter or olive oil

- 1 stalk celery or 1 small green bell pepper, chopped

- 1 teaspoon ground black pepper

- A handful fresh parsley, minced

**Directions:**

1. Rinse the tomatoes well. Remove any stem or leaves from the tomatoes. Cut tomatoes into 4 quarters each and place them in a large saucepan. Place the saucepan over medium-high heat.

2. Wait for it to come to a boil. Make sure to stir often.

3. Lower the heat and cook for about 15 – 18 minutes. As it cooks, stir periodically so that the tomatoes do not get stuck on the bottom of the saucepan. Turn off the heat and spoon the tomatoes into a food mill or strainer in batches and strain the tomatoes. Discard the solids remaining in the food mill.

4. Pour the strained tomatoes into the saucepan. Place the saucepan over medium heat and cook until it is reduced to about half its original quantity or to the thickness you desire.

5. Meanwhile, place a pan over medium heat. Add butter or oil. When butter melts, add onion, celery, garlic, and mushrooms and cook for 5 – 6 minutes until vegetables are slightly tender.

6. Turn off the heat and transfer the sautéed vegetables into the saucepan containing tomato sauce.

7. Stir in pepper, oregano, salt, sugar, and parsley. Stir often until sugar dissolves completely.

8. Lower the heat and let it simmer on low heat to keep warm.

9. While the sauce is cooking, during the last 30 minutes, arrange the pressure canner, canning lids, and jars. You need about three to four 1 pint jars (500 ml). Pour enough water into the pressure canner following the manufacturer's instructions such that it is about 3 inches (8 centimeters) in height from the bottom of the canner. Place the canner on your stovetop over low heat. Place the jars in the canner so that the jars remain warm. The temperature of the water in the canner should be maintained at 180°F (82°C). Place the lids in a small saucepan of water over low heat on another burner.

10. Take out the jars from the canner with the help of the canning tongs. Place the funnel on top of the jar. Spoon the tomato sauce into the jars until you get a headspace of 1 inch (2.5 cm).

11. Make sure to remove bubbles using a bubble removing tool. Reassess the headspace. On reassessing, if the headspace increases, add some more sauce.

12. Take a clean damp cloth and wipe the rim of the jars. Place the canning lid on each jar using the lid lifter. Place the canning ring on each jar and tighten it as suggested.

13. Place the jars in the canner and process the jars following the manufacturer's instruction manual at 5 psi (36 kPa). Set the timer for 20 minutes for sea level. The timing will be 50 minutes at 6 psi (41 kPa) between 1,001 to 3,000 feet. The timing will be 55 minutes at 7 psi (48 kPa) between 3,001 to 6,000 feet. The timing will be 60 minutes at 8 psi (55 kPa) for above 6,001 feet. Once the timer goes off, turn off the burner.

14. Once you are done with the processing, let the pressure release naturally before opening the canner and taking out the jars. Let the jars cool completely on your countertop for no less than 12 hours. Wipe the jars with a dry kitchen cloth or paper towel. Make sure to check for the seals. These jars will last you for 12 to 18 months.

15. **Serving suggestion**: You can use spaghetti sauce in numerous dishes like curries, pasta, pizzas, soups, braised meat etc. to make it more flavorful.

# Tomato Sauce

Makes: 4 – 5 pint jars (500 ml) or 2 – 3 quart jars (1 L)

**Ingredients:**

For thick tomato sauce:

- 14 pounds whole tomatoes for pint size jars or 23 pounds tomatoes for quart size jars

- ½ teaspoon salt per pint size jar or 1 teaspoon salt per quart size jar (optional)

- Seasoning blend to taste

For thin tomato sauce:
- 10.5 pounds whole tomatoes for pint size jars or 17.5 pounds tomatoes for quart size jars
- ½ teaspoon salt per pint size jar or 1 teaspoon salt per quart size jar (optional)
- Seasoning blend to taste

**Use any one of these acidic ingredients: This is important, whether for thick sauce or thin sauce.**
- 1 tablespoon lemon juice per pint size jar or 2 tablespoons lemon juice per quart size jar (bottled lemon juice)
- ¼ teaspoon citric acid per pint size jar or ½ teaspoon citric acid per quart size jar

**Seasoning blend variations:**

Creole seasoning blend:
- 2 tablespoons hot paprika
- 2 tablespoons dried oregano
- 4 teaspoons onion powder
- 4 teaspoons dried thyme
- 2 teaspoons ground white pepper
- 2 tablespoons sweet paprika
- 2 tablespoons ground red pepper
- 4 teaspoons garlic powder
- 4 teaspoons ground black pepper
- 2 teaspoons celery seeds

Mexican seasoning blend:

- 4 teaspoons garlic powder

- 4 teaspoons dried oregano

- 8 teaspoons chili powder

- 8 teaspoons ground chipotle pepper

- 4 teaspoons coriander seeds

- 4 teaspoons cumin seeds

Italian seasoning blend:

- 4 teaspoons dried crushed red pepper

- 2 tablespoons garlic powder

- 4 tablespoons dried oregano

- 4 teaspoons dried thyme

- 4 teaspoons dried basil

**Directions:**

1. To make seasoning blend: You will need to add more seasoning blend to make thin sauce and lesser seasoning blend for thick sauce. You can always add enough to suit your taste.

2. To make creole seasoning blend and Italian seasoning blend, simply gather the ingredients and mix them together in a bowl.

3. To make Mexican seasoning blend, add coriander and cumin seeds into a dry pan and place the pan over medium-low heat. Toast the spices until you get a nice aroma. Turn

off the heat and let it cool for a few minutes. Powder the spices in a spice grinder or in a mortar using a pestle.

4. Add the ground spices into a bowl along with the rest of the ingredients and mix well. Rinse the tomatoes well. Remove any stem or leaves from the tomatoes.

5. Cut about a pound of tomatoes, each into four quarters, and place them in a large saucepan.

6. Place the saucepan over high heat. Continue quartering the tomatoes about a pound at a time and keep adding them to the pot. Be quick while cutting and adding.

7. Stir as you add tomatoes and mash the tomatoes with the back of a large stirring spoon or potato masher. When all the tomatoes are added, wait for it to come to a boil. Make sure to stir often. Lower the heat and cook for about five minutes. As it cooks, stir often so that the tomatoes do not get stuck on the bottom of the saucepan.

8. Turn off the heat and spoon the tomatoes into a food mill or strainer in batches and strain the tomatoes. Discard the solids remaining in the food mill. Pour the strained tomatoes into the saucepan. Add the seasoning blend now and stir.

9. Place the saucepan over medium heat and cook until the sauce reduces to 2/3 of the strained mixture for thin sauce. Cook until the sauce reduces to ½ the strained mixture for thick sauce.

10. While the tomato sauce is cooking, arrange the pressure canner, canning lids, and jars. You need four to five 1 pint jars (500 ml) or two to three quart size jars (1 L). Pour enough water into the pressure canner following the manufacturer's instructions such that it is about 3 inches (8 centimeters) in height from the bottom of the canner. Place the canner on your stovetop over low heat. Place the jars in the canner so that the jars remain warm. The temperature of the water in the canner should be maintained at 180°F (82°C). Place the lids in a small saucepan of water over low heat on another burner.

11. Place the jars on a towel on your countertop. Add citric acid and lemon juice into each jar. Place a funnel over the jars. Spoon the tomato sauce into the jars until you get a headspace of ¼ inch (0.6 cm).

12. Make sure to remove bubbles using a bubble removing tool. Reassess the headspace. On reassessing, if the headspace increases, add some more tomato sauce.

13. Take a clean damp cloth and wipe the rim of the jars. Place the canning lid on each jar using the lid lifter. Place the canning ring on each jar and tighten it as suggested.

14. Place the jars in the canner and process the jars following the manufacturer's instruction manual at 5 psi (36 kPa). Set the timer for 20 minutes for sea level. The timing will be 50 minutes at 6 psi (41 kPa) between 1,001 to 3,000 feet. The timing will be 55 minutes at 7 psi (48 kPa) between 3,001 to 6,000 feet. The timing will be 60 minutes at 8 psi (55 kPa) for above 6,001 feet. Once the timer goes off, turn off the burner.

15. Once you are done with the processing, let the pressure release naturally before opening the canner and taking out the jars. Let the jars cool completely on your countertop for no less than 12 hours. Wipe the jars with a dry kitchen cloth or paper towel. Make sure to check for the seals. These jars will last you for 12 to 18 months.

16. **Serving suggestion**: You can use tomato paste in numerous dishes like curries, pasta sauce, soups, braised meat etc. to make it more flavorful.

# Chapter 5:
# Meat

## Pork

Makes: 6 pint jars (500 ml)

**Ingredients:**

- 4.4 pounds (2 kg) pork butt

- 3 teaspoons (15 g) kosher salt

- 1 teaspoon (5 g) Cure #1

- 1 teaspoon (5 g) ground allspice

- Two cloves garlic, minced

- 1 tablespoon (15 g) caramelized onion per jar

- 1 teaspoon (5 g) ground black pepper

- One bay leaf per jar

Serving instructions per 1 pint jar (500 ml):

- Grated cheese

- Chopped fresh herbs of your choice

- Butter

**Directions:**

1. Trim the pork of extra fat and chop into 1 inch chunks and place in a large bowl.

2. To cure the meat: Combine salt and cure #1 in a bowl and sprinkle the salt mixture over the meat. Toss well. Cover the bowl with cling wrap and place it in the refrigerator for a minimum of 24 hours and a maximum of 48 hours.

3. Once you are done with curing, arrange the pressure canner, canning lids, and jars. You need six 1 pint jars (500 ml). Pour enough water into the pressure canner following the manufacturer's instructions such that it is about 3 inches (8 centimeters) in height from the bottom of the canner. Place the canner on your stovetop over low heat. Place the jars in the canner so that the jars remain warm. The temperature of the water in the canner should be maintained at 180°F (82°C). Place the lids in a small saucepan of water over low heat on another burner.

4. Add pepper, allspice, and garlic into the bowl of pork and stir until well combined. Place the jars over a towel on your countertop. It is better to use a funnel while pouring the meat into the jars. Add meat into the jars until you get a headspace of 1 inch (2.5 cm). Pack the meat in the jars but do not pack very tightly. Place a bay leaf in each jar. Place a tablespoon of caramelized onion in each jar.

5. No water or broth is to be added to the jars and the meat will leave its liquid on pressure canning.

6. Make sure to remove bubbles using a bubble removing tool. Reassess the headspace and add more meat if required to fill up to the required headspace.

7. Take a clean damp cloth and wipe the rim of the jars. Place the canning lid on each jar using the lid lifter. Place the canning ring on each jar and tighten it as suggested.

8. Place the jars in the canner and process the jars following the manufacturer's instruction manual at 15 psi (103 kPa). Set the timer for 65 to 70 minutes depending on how you like the meat cooked, adjusting for altitude if required. Once the timer goes off, turn off the burner. I prefer to cook it for 70 minutes.

9.  Once you are done with the processing, let the pressure release naturally before opening the canner and taking out the jars. Let the jars cool completely on your countertop for no less than 12 hours. Wipe the jars with a dry kitchen cloth or paper towel. Make sure to check for the seals. These jars will last you for about 12 months.

10. **Serving suggestion**: Empty the contents of a jar into a saucepan. Heat over medium heat on your stovetop. Discard the bay leaf. Ladle into bowls. Add some salt and pepper to taste if desired. Add a blob of butter in each bowl. Garnish with cheese and any other fresh herbs of your choice and serve.

# Pulled Pork Barbecue

Makes: 6 pint jars (500 ml)

**Ingredients:**

- 7 pounds (3.2 kg) pork butt (barbequed or cooked in a slow cooker)

- 2 quarts (2 L) beef stock or water

- 2 pints (4 L) BBQ or more to taste

For BBQ sauce:

- 3 ¾ cups (830 ml) ketchup

- ½ cup (110 g) brown sugar

- ½ cup (110 g) prepared mustard

- ½ cup (125 ml) apple cider vinegar

- 2 teaspoons (10 g) ground black pepper

- 2 tablespoons (30 ml) Worcestershire sauce

- 1 tablespoon (15 ml) lemon juice

- 1 tablespoon (15 g) garlic powder

- 1 tablespoon (15 ml) liquid smoke

- 2 tablespoons (30 ml) hot sauce

Serving instructions per 1 pint jar (500 ml):

- Burger buns or tortillas

- Toppings of your choice

- Grated cheese

- Chopped fresh herbs of your choice

**Directions:**

1. You can cook the pork in a BBQ or in a slow cooker or as you normally cook. In case you have cooked the pork in a BBQ, use only ½ tablespoon (7.5 ml) of the liquid smoke. Now pull the pork with a pair of forks and add into a large stock pot.

2. Arrange the pressure canner, canning lids, and jars. You need about six 1 pint (500 ml) size jars. Pour enough water into the pressure canner following the manufacturer's instructions such that it is about 3 inches (8 centimeters) in height from the bottom of the canner. Place the canner on your stovetop over low heat. Place the jars in the canner so that the jars remain warm. The temperature of the water in the canner should be maintained at 180°F (82°C). Place the lids in a small saucepan of water over low heat on another burner.

3. Boil water or stock in a pot.

4. Combine all the BBQ sauce ingredients in a large stock pot. Stir until well combined. Add the pulled pork and place the pot over high heat. Bring to a boil, stirring often. If the sauce is not coating well over the pork, you can add some water.

5. Distribute the meat among the jars. Pour enough boiling water into the jars until you get headspace of 1 inch (2.5 cm)

6. Make sure to remove bubbles using a bubble removing tool. Reassess the headspace and add more water if required to fill up to the required headspace.

7. Take a clean damp cloth and wipe the rim of the jars. Place the canning lid on each jar using the lid lifter. Place the canning ring on each jar and tighten it as suggested.

8. Place the jars in the canner and process the jars following the manufacturer's instruction manual at 10 psi (69 kPa). Set the timer for 65 minutes adjusting for altitude if required. Once the timer goes off, turn off the burner.

9. Once you are done with the processing, let the pressure release naturally before opening the canner and taking out the jars. Let the jars cool completely on your countertop for no less than 12 hours. Wipe the jars with a dry kitchen cloth or paper towel. Make sure to check for the seals. These jars will last you for about 12 months.

10. **Serving suggestion**: Empty the contents of the jar into a pan and heat thoroughly. Serve over burger buns or over tortillas or over lettuce leaves with cheese and toppings of your choice.

# Pork Meatballs

Makes: 8 – 9 pint jars (500 ml) or 4 – 5 quart jars (1 L)

**Ingredients:**
- 4 pounds (1.8 kg) ground pork
- 1 teaspoon (5 g) ground black pepper
- 4 teaspoons (20 g) garlic powder
- 2 teaspoons (10 g) dried thyme

- 2 teaspoons (10 g) ground cumin

- 2 teaspoons (10 g) ground coriander

- 4 teaspoons (20 g) onion powder

- 4 teaspoons (20 g) sweet paprika

- 4 teaspoons (20 g) kosher salt

- Water, stock or tomato juice, as required

Serving instructions per serving of 2 meatballs:

- Pasta sauce of your choice

- Hot cooked pasta or rice

**Directions:**

1. Combine pork, salt, and spices in a bowl. Make small balls of the mixture of about 3 inches (7.5 cm) each. I suggest you dip your hands often in water and make the meatballs. This way the meat will not stick to your hands. Make sure you do not add any binders like egg or breadcrumbs.

2. Arrange the pressure canner, canning lids, and jars. You need about eight to nine 1 pint (500 ml) size jars or four to five quart (1 L) size jars. Pour enough water into the pressure canner following the manufacturer's instructions such that it is about 3 inches (8 centimeters) in height from the bottom of the canner. Place the canner on your stovetop over low heat. Place the jars in the canner so that the jars remain warm. The temperature of the water in the canner should be maintained at 180°F (82°C). Place the lids in a small saucepan of water over low heat on another burner.

3. Boil water or stock or tomato stock in a pot.

4. Place a skillet over medium heat. Spray some cooking spray into the skillet. Add a few meatballs into the pan without overcrowding. And cook until brown all over. It should not be cooked through as it will be cooked further while processing. Remove the

meatballs from the pan and make sure to keep them warm until the remaining meatballs are browned.

5.  Place the jars over a towel on your countertop. Place meatballs in the jar. Pack them loosely. Pour enough boiling liquid into the jars until you get headspace of 1 inch (2.5 cm).

6.  Make sure to remove bubbles using a bubble removing tool. Reassess the headspace and add more boiling liquid if required to fill up to the required head pace.

7.  Take a clean damp cloth and wipe the rim of the jars. Place the canning lid on each jar using the lid lifter. Place the canning ring on each jar and tighten it as suggested.

8.  Place the jars in the canner and process the jars following the manufacturer's instruction manual at 10 psi (69 kPa). Set the timer for 75 minutes for a pint-sized (500 ml) jar or 90 minutes for a quart-sized (1 L) jars adjusting for altitude if required. Once the timer goes off, turn off the burner.

9.  Once you are done with the processing, let the pressure release naturally before opening the canner and taking out the jars. Let the jars cool completely on your countertop for no less than 12 hours. Wipe the jars with a dry kitchen cloth or paper towel. Make sure to check for the seals. These jars will last you for about 12 months.

10. **Serving suggestion**: Add some pasta sauce into a pan and let it heat over medium heat. Add the meatballs and heat thoroughly. Serve over hot cooked pasta or rice.

# Hamburger Patties

Makes: 4 quart jars (1 L)

**Ingredients:**

- 6 pounds (1.8 kg) ground beef or pork

- One bell pepper, diced

- Two onions, diced

- 2 tablespoons (30 g) ranch dressing

- 2 tablespoons (30 g) beef bouillon

- 2 tablespoons (30 g) seasoned salt

- 2 tablespoons (30 ml) Worcestershire sauce

- Boiling water or stock or tomato juice as required

Serving instructions per burger:
- One burger bun

- One lettuce leaf

- One cheese slice (optional)

- Any other toppings of your choice

**Directions:**

1. Combine meat, onion, bell pepper, Worcestershire sauce, ranch dressing, and seasoned salt in a large bowl. Make sure you do not use any binders like eggs or breadcrumbs.

2. Make patties of the meat mixture such that they are as wide as the mouth of the jar and they fit well into the jars. You can use your hands to shape the patties. You can also use the help of the canning rings to shape the burgers. You should use a wide mouth jar to can the burgers. You can cook the patties in a pan or in an oven. They only need to be browned and not cooked through inside.

3. To cook them in the oven, place the patties on a baking sheet and bake them in an oven that has been preheated to 375°F for about 15 minutes on each side.

4. If you are cooking them in batches, make sure the burgers are kept warm until you place them in the jars.

5.  While the burgers are cooking, arrange the pressure canner, canning lids, and jars. You need about four quart (1 L) size jars. Pour enough water into the pressure canner following the manufacturer's instructions such that it is about 3 inches (8 centimeters) in height from the bottom of the canner. Place the canner on your stovetop over low heat. Place the jars in the canner so that the jars remain warm. The temperature of the water in the canner should be maintained at 180°F (82°C). Place the lids in a small saucepan of water over low heat on another burner.

6.  Place a kitchen towel on your countertop and spread it. Lift the jars from the canner and place over the towel. Place the burgers in the jars. Pour the chosen boiling liquid into the jars to cover the burgers leaving headspace of 1 inch (2.5 cm).

7.  Make sure to remove bubbles using a bubble removing tool. Reassess the headspace and add more liquid if required to fill up to the required headspace.

8.  Take a clean damp cloth and wipe the rim of the jars. Place the canning lid on each jar using the lid lifter. Place the canning ring on each jar and tighten it as suggested.

9.  Place the jars in the canner and process the jars following the manufacturer's instruction manual at 10 psi (69 kPa). Set the timer for 90 minutes, adjusting for altitude if required. Once the timer goes off, turn off the burner.

10. Once you are done with the processing, let the pressure release naturally before opening the canner and taking out the jars. Let the jars cool completely on your countertop for no less than 12 hours. Wipe the jars with a dry kitchen cloth or paper towel. Make sure to check for the seals. These jars will last you for about 12 months.

11. **Serving suggestion**: Take out a burger from the jar and place on a hot pan over medium heat. You can spray some oil into the pan before placing the burger and cook until crisp on both the sides. Split the bun into two and lightly toast the bun. Place a lettuce leaf over the bottom half of the bun followed by the burger and a slice of cheese. Place any other topping or sauce of your choice. Cover with the top half of the bun and serve.

# Venison

Makes: 5 pint jars (500 ml)

## Ingredients:

- 5 pounds lean venison, cubed

- 1 ¼ teaspoons ground black pepper

- 20 slices onion

- 5 teaspoons salt

- 5 teaspoons minced garlic

- 5 tablespoons minced green bell pepper (optional)

Serving instructions per 1 pint jar (500 ml):

- Chopped parsley

## Directions:

1. Arrange the pressure canner, canning lids, and jars. You need about five 1 pint (500 ml) size jars. Pour enough water into the pressure canner following the manufacturer's instructions such that it is about 3 inches (8 centimeters) in height from the bottom of the canner. Place the canner on your stovetop over low heat. Place the jars in the canner so that the jars remain warm. The temperature of the water in the canner should be maintained at 180°F (82°C). Place the lids in a small saucepan of water over low heat on another burner.

2. Meanwhile, combine meat, salt, garlic, and pepper in a large bowl.

3. Place a kitchen towel on your countertop and spread it. Lift the jars from the canner and place over the towel.

4. Fill the jars with the meat, leaving a headspace of ½ inch (1.25 cm). Do not pack the meat very tightly. Add five slices of onion and 1 tablespoon of green bell pepper into each jar. No water or broth needs to be added to the jars as the meat will leave enough liquid on pressure canning.

5. Make sure to remove bubbles using a bubble removing tool. Reassess the headspace and add more meat if required to fill up to the required headspace.

6. Take a clean damp cloth and wipe the rim of the jars. Place the canning lid on each jar using the lid lifter. Place the canning ring on each jar and tighten it as suggested.

7. Place the jars in the canner and process the jars following the manufacturer's instruction manual at 10 psi (69 kPa). Set the timer for 75 minutes, adjusting for altitude if required. Once the timer goes off, turn off the burner.

8. Once you are done with the processing, let the pressure release naturally before opening the canner and taking out the jars. Let the jars cool completely on your countertop for no less than 12 hours. Wipe the jars with a dry kitchen cloth or paper towel. Make sure to check for the seals. These jars will last you for about 12 months.

9. **Serving suggestion**: Empty the contents of the jar into a pan and heat thoroughly. Transfer into a bowl. Garnish with parsley and serve. You can serve this as it is or serve it as a filling for sandwiches. You can also add the meat to stews or chilies.

# Sausage

Makes: 6 pint jars (500 ml)

**Ingredients:**

- 4 pounds sausage links, cut into desired size

- Boiling stock or water or tomato juice

Serving instructions per 1 pint jar (500 ml):

- Two eggs

- Salt and pepper to taste

- Grated cheese to taste (optional)

**Directions:**

1. Arrange the pressure canner, canning lids, and jars. You need six 1 pint (500 ml) size jars. Pour enough water into the pressure canner following the manufacturer's instructions such that it is about 3 inches (8 centimeters) in height from the bottom of the canner. Place the canner on your stovetop over low heat. Place the jars in the canner so that the jars remain warm. The temperature of the water in the canner should be maintained at 180°F (82°C). Place the lids in a small saucepan of water over low heat on another burner.

2. Place a pan over high heat. When the pan is hot, add sausage links and cook until brown. Place a kitchen towel on your countertop and spread it. Lift the jars from the canner and place over the towel.

3. Fill the jars with the sausage pieces making sure to divide them equally. Pour boiling liquid into the jars to cover the sausages leaving headspace of 1 inch (2.5 cm).

4. Make sure to remove bubbles using a bubble removing tool. Reassess the headspace and add more liquid if required to fill up to the required headspace.

5. Take a clean damp cloth and wipe the rim of the jars. Place the canning lid on each jar using the lid lifter. Place the canning ring on each jar and tighten it as suggested.

6. Place the jars in the canner and process the jars following the manufacturer's instruction manual at 10 psi (69 kPa). Set the timer for 90 minutes, adjusting for altitude if required. Once the timer goes off, turn off the burner.

7. Once you are done with the processing, let the pressure release naturally before opening the canner and taking out the jars. Let the jars cool completely on your countertop for no less than 12 hours. Wipe the jars with a dry kitchen cloth or paper towel. Make sure to check for the seals. These jars will last you for about 12 months.

8. **Serving suggestion**: Grease a microwave bowl with some oil. Add sausage and heat for a couple of minutes. Add beaten eggs, salt, and pepper and stir. Cook for about a minute in the microwave until the eggs are cooked. Make sure to stir the mixture every 15 to 17 seconds. Serve hot. You can use the sausages in different ways like in making egg muffins, adding to breakfast hash, frittatas, soups, stews, etc.

# Beef Stew

Makes: 6 pint jars (500 ml)

**Ingredients:**

- 2.5 pounds (1.1 kg) beef stew meat, cut into 1 ½ inch (3.8 cm) cubes

- Three medium carrots, peeled**Error! Bookmark not defined.**, sliced

- 3 teaspoons (15 g) sea salt

- Boiling water or broth, as required

- Five medium-large potatoes, peeled, cut into cubes

- 1 ½ large onions, diced

- Pepper to taste (optional)

<u>Serving instructions per 1 pint jar (500 ml):</u>

- Hot cooked rice or noodles

- Side dish of your choice

## Directions:

1. Arrange the pressure canner, canning lids, and jars. You need six 1 pint (500 ml) size jars. Pour enough water into the pressure canner following the manufacturer's instructions such that it is about 3 inches (8 centimeters) in height from the bottom of the canner. Place the canner on your stovetop over low heat. Place the jars in the canner so that the jars remain warm. The temperature of the water in the canner should be maintained at 180°F (82°C). Place the lids in a small saucepan of water over low heat on another burner.

2. Boil a pot of water or broth.

3. Place a kitchen towel on your countertop and spread it. Lift the jars from the canner and place over the towel.

4. Fill the jars with meat, potatoes, carrots, and onions. Make sure they are equally distributed. Add ½ teaspoon salt into each jar. Add pepper to taste if desired. Pour boiling liquid into the jars to cover the meat and vegetables leaving headspace of 1 inch (2.5 cm).

5. Make sure to remove bubbles using a bubble removing tool. Reassess the headspace and add more liquid if required to fill up to the required headspace.

6. Take a clean damp cloth and wipe the rim of the jars. Place the canning lid on each jar using the lid lifter. Place the canning ring on each jar and tighten it as suggested.

7. Place the jars in the canner and process the jars following the manufacturer's instruction manual at 10 psi (69 kPa). Set the timer for 75 minutes, adjusting for altitude if required. Once the timer goes off, turn off the burner.

8. Once you are done with the processing, let the pressure release naturally before opening the canner and taking out the jars. Let the jars cool completely on your countertop for

no less than 12 hours. Wipe the jars with a dry kitchen cloth or paper towel. Make sure to check for the seals. These jars will last you for about 12 months.

9. **Serving suggestion**: Empty the contents of a jar into a saucepan and heat it thoroughly. Serve over hot cooked rice or noodles with a side dish like green beans.

# Sloppy Joe Filling

Makes: 12 pint jars (500 ml) or 6 quart jars (1 L)

## Ingredients:

- 8 pounds (3.6 kg) ground chuck

- Two medium green bell peppers, diced

- 4 tablespoons (60 ml) Worcestershire sauce

- 1 cup (250 ml) water

- ½ cup (125 ml) apple cider vinegar

- 2 teaspoons (10 g) salt

- Three medium onions, diced

- 6-8 large cloves garlic, peeled, minced

- 6 cups (1.5 L) ketchup

- ½ cup (110 g) brown sugar

- 2 tablespoons (30 g) mustard

Serving instructions per 1 pint jar (500 ml):

- Cheese slices

- Burger buns

**Directions:**

1. Arrange the pressure canner, canning lids, and jars. You need about twelve 1 pint (500 ml) size jars or six quart (1 L) size jars. Pour enough water into the pressure canner following the manufacturer's instructions such that it is about 3 inches (8 centimeters) in height from the bottom of the canner. Place the canner on your stovetop over low heat. Place the jars in the canner so that the jars remain warm. The temperature of the water in the canner should be maintained at 180°F (82°C). Place the lids in a small saucepan of water over low heat on another burner.

2. Put the onions and meat into a large stockpot and cook the mixture over medium-high heat until the meat is brown. Drain off as much fat as possible. Add bell pepper, garlic, water, vinegar, salt, ketchup, brown sugar, and mustard and mix well. When the mixture starts boiling, lower the heat and cook for about 20 minutes, stirring often.

3. Place a kitchen towel on your countertop and spread it. Lift the jars from the canner and place over the towel.

4. Fill the jars with the meat mixture leaving a headspace of 1 inch (2.5 cm).

5. Make sure to remove bubbles using a bubble removing tool. Reassess the headspace and add more meat mixture if required to fill up to the required headspace.

6. Take a clean damp cloth and wipe the rim of the jars. Place the canning lid on each jar using the lid lifter. Place the canning ring on each jar and tighten it as suggested.

7. Place the jars in the canner and process the jars following the manufacturer's instruction manual at 10 psi (69 kPa). Set the timer for 75 minutes for pint size (500 ml) or 90 minutes for quart (1 L) size, adjusting for altitude if required. Once the timer goes off, turn off the burner.

8. Once you are done with the processing, let the pressure release naturally before opening the canner and taking out the jars. Let the jars cool completely on your countertop for no less than 12 hours. Wipe the jars with a dry kitchen cloth or paper towel. Make sure to check for the seals. These jars will last you for about 12 months.

9. **Serving suggestion**: Empty the contents of the jar into a pan and heat thoroughly. Serve over burger buns with a slice or 2 of cheese.

# Un-Stuffed Cabbage Rolls

Makes: 12 quart jars (1 L)

**Ingredients:**

- 4 pounds (1.8 kg) ground chuck

- 4-6 large cloves garlic, minced

- Two medium cabbages, cored, chopped

- 1 pound (454 g) mushrooms, halved or quartered depending on the size

- 2 cups (500 ml) water

- 4 teaspoons (20 g) ground black pepper

- Two large onions, chopped

- 2 cups (256 g) julienne cut carrots

- 4 cups (720 g) chopped tomatoes

- 4 cups (1 L) tomato sauce

- 4 teaspoons (20 g) salt

Serving instructions per 1 quart jar (1 L):

- Cucumber salad or bean salad (optional)

- Roasted potatoes or mashed potatoes

**Directions:**

1.  Arrange the pressure canner, canning lids, and jars. You need about twelve quart (1 L) size jars. Pour enough water into the pressure canner following the manufacturer's instructions such that it is about 3 inches (8 centimeters) in height from the bottom of the canner. Place the canner on your stovetop over low heat. Place the jars in the canner so that the jars remain warm. The temperature of the water in the canner should be maintained at 180°F (82°C). Place the lids in a small saucepan of water over low heat on another burner.

2.  Put the onions and meat into a large stockpot and cook the mixture over medium-high heat until the meat is brown. Drain off as much fat as possible. Add cabbage, carrots, mushrooms, tomatoes, garlic, water, salt, and tomato sauce and mix well. When the mixture starts boiling, lower the heat and cook for 3-4 minutes, until cabbage wilts slightly, stirring often.

3.  Place a kitchen towel on your countertop and spread it. Lift the jars from the canner and place over the towel.

4.  Fill the jars with the meat mixture leaving a headspace of 1 inch (2.5 cm).

5.  Make sure to remove bubbles using a bubble removing tool. Reassess the headspace and add more meat mixture if required to fill up to the required headspace.

6.  Take a clean damp cloth and wipe the rim of the jars. Place the canning lid on each jar using the lid lifter. Place the canning ring on each jar and tighten it as suggested.

7.  Place the jars in the canner and process the jars following the manufacturer's instruction manual at 10 psi (69 kPa). Set the timer for 90 minutes for quart (1 L) size, adjusting for altitude if required. Once the timer goes off, turn off the burner.

8.  Once you are done with the processing, let the pressure release naturally before opening the canner and taking out the jars. Let the jars cool completely on your countertop for no less than 12 hours. Wipe the jars with a dry kitchen cloth or paper towel. Make sure to check for the seals. These jars will last you for about 12 months.

9. **Serving suggestion**: Empty the contents of the jar into a pan and heat thoroughly. Serve along with any one of the suggested side dishes for a complete meal.

# Corned Beef and Potatoes

Makes: 4 – 5 quart jars (1 L)

**Ingredients:**

- 8–10 pounds (3.6–4.5 kg) beef brisket, home cured or pre-cured package

- ¼ teaspoon (1.25 g) pickling spice per quart (1 L) size jar

- 10–12 russet potatoes, scrubbed, peeled, cut into 1 inch cubes

- 4–5 carrots (optional), peeled, cut into 1 inch cubes

- Boiling water as required

<u>Serving instructions per 1 quart jar (1 L):</u>

- Favorite salad of your choice

## Directions:

1. Arrange the pressure canner, canning lids, and jars. You need about four to five quart (1 L) size jars. Pour enough water into the pressure canner following the manufacturer's instructions such that it is about 3 inches (8 centimeters) in height from the bottom of the canner. Place the canner on your stovetop over low heat. Place the jars in the canner so that the jars remain warm. The temperature of the water in the canner should be maintained at 180°F (82°C). Place the lids in a small saucepan of water over low heat on another burner.

2. Boil a pot or kettle of water.

3. Trim the fat from the briskets and chop into 1 inch chunks.

4. Place a kitchen towel on your countertop and spread it. Lift the jars from the canner and place over the towel. Add pickling spice into each jar.

5. First divide the meat among the jars. Layer with equal amount of potatoes and carrots in each jar. Fill the jars with the boiling water covering the meat, leaving a headspace of 1 inch (2.5 cm).

6. Make sure to remove bubbles using a bubble removing tool. Reassess the headspace and add more water if required to fill up to the required headspace.

7. Take a clean damp cloth and wipe the rim of the jars. Place the canning lid on each jar using the lid lifter. Place the canning ring on each jar and tighten it as suggested.

8. Place the jars in the canner and process the jars following the manufacturer's instruction manual at 10 psi (69 kPa). Set the timer for 90 minutes for quart (1 L) size, adjusting for altitude if required. Once the timer goes off, turn off the burner.

9. Once you are done with the processing, let the pressure release naturally before opening the canner and taking out the jars. Let the jars cool completely on your countertop for

no less than 12 hours. Wipe the jars with a dry kitchen cloth or paper towel. Make sure to check for the seals. These jars will last you for about 12 months.

10. **Serving suggestion**: Empty the contents of the jar into a pan and heat thoroughly. Serve along with your favorite salad for a complete meal. If there is not particularly a favorite salad of your choice, here are a few suggestions apart from salads that go well like potato gratin, dinner rolls, roasted red potatoes, marinated artichoke hearts etc.

# Burrito in a Jar

Makes: 4 quart jars (1 L)

**Ingredients:**

- 1 cup (171 g) dried pinto beans

- One large green bell pepper, diced

- 2 pounds (907 g) ground beef

- 2 tablespoons (30 g) taco seasoning

- Beef broth, as required

- Two medium onions, diced

- ½ cup (125 g) Rotel tomatoes

- 1 teaspoon (5 g) salt

Serving instructions per 1 quart jar (1 L):

- 1 cup cooked rice

- Tortillas

- Lettuce

- Tomatoes

- Any other favorite toppings of your choice

**Directions:**

1. Arrange the pressure canner, canning lids, and jars. You need about four quart (1 L) size jars. Pour enough water into the pressure canner following the manufacturer's instructions such that it is about 3 inches (8 centimeters) in height from the bottom of the canner. Place the canner on your stovetop over low heat. Place the jars in the canner so that the jars remain warm. The temperature of the water in the canner should be maintained at 180°F (82°C). Place the lids in a small saucepan of water over low heat on another burner.

2. Put the meat into a large stockpot and cook the mixture over medium-high heat until the meat is brown. Turn off the heat. Drain off as much fat as possible. Boil stock in a pot.

3.  Place a kitchen towel on your countertop and spread it. Lift the jars from the canner and place over the towel.

4.  You need to place the ingredients in layers. It looks so very nice and tempting. First divide the dried beans among the jars. Layer with equal amount of bell peppers in each jar followed by onions. Next layer with equal quantities of beef in each jar followed by tomatoes. Sprinkle ½ tablespoon taco seasoning and ¼ teaspoon salt in each jar. Fill the jars with the boiling stock to cover the ingredients, leaving a headspace of 1 inch (2.5 cm).

5.  Make sure to remove bubbles using a bubble removing tool. Reassess the headspace and add more liquid if required to fill up to the required headspace.

6.  Take a clean damp cloth and wipe the rim of the jars. Place the canning lid on each jar using the lid lifter. Place the canning ring on each jar and tighten it as suggested.

7.  Place the jars in the canner and process the jars following the manufacturer's instruction manual at 10 psi (69 kPa). Set the timer for 90 minutes for quart (1 L) size, adjusting for altitude if required. Once the timer goes off, turn off the burner.

8.  Once you are done with the processing, let the pressure release naturally before opening the canner and taking out the jars. Let the jars cool completely on your countertop for no less than 12 hours. Wipe the jars with a dry kitchen cloth or paper towel. Make sure to check for the seals. These jars will last you for about 12 months.

9.  **Serving suggestion**: Empty the contents of the jar into a pan. Add cooked rice and heat thoroughly. Heat up the tortillas following the instructions given on the package. Top the burrito mixture over tortillas. Top with lettuce, tomatoes, and any other favorite burrito toppings of your choice and serve.

# Chicken and Gravy

Makes: 8 pint jars (500 ml) or 4 quart jars (1 L)

**Ingredients**

- 2 cups (350 g) chopped onion

- 2 cups (350 g) peeled, diced potatoes

- 2 cups (250 g) finely chopped celery

- 4 pounds (1.8 kg) boneless chicken, cut into 2 inch (5 cm) chunks

- 4 teaspoons (20 g) poultry seasoning

- 4 teaspoons (20 g) salt

- 2 teaspoons (10 g) ground black pepper

- Boiling chicken stock or water, as required

- 8 tablespoons (118 ml) dry white wine

Serving instructions per 1 pint jar (500 ml):

- Chopped parsley

- 1 tablespoon (15 g) cornstarch mixed with ¼ cup (125 ml) water

- Hot cooked rice

**Directions:**

1. Arrange the pressure canner, canning lids, and jars. You need eight 1 pint (500 ml) size jars or four quart size (1 L) jars. Pour enough water into the pressure canner following the manufacturer's instructions such that it is about 3 inches (8 centimeters) in height from the bottom of the canner. Place the canner on your stovetop over low heat. Place the jars in the canner so that the jars remain warm. The temperature of the water in the

canner should be maintained at 180°F (82°C). Place the lids in a small saucepan of water over low heat on another burner.

2. Boil a pot of water or broth. Meanwhile, combine chicken, potatoes, celery, and onions in a bowl.

3. Place a kitchen towel on your countertop and spread it. Lift the jars from the canner and place over the towel. Pack the mixture into the jars using a funnel. They should be firmly packed and not tightly packed. Pour boiling liquid into the jars to cover the mixture leaving a headspace of 1 inch (2.5 cm).

4. Make sure to remove bubbles using a bubble removing tool. Reassess the headspace and add more liquid if required to fill up to the required headspace.

5. Take a clean damp cloth and wipe the rim of the jars. Place the canning lid on each jar using the lid lifter. Place the canning ring on each jar and tighten it as suggested.

6. Place the jars in the canner and process the jars following the manufacturer's instruction manual at 10 psi (69 kPa). Set the timer for 75 minutes, adjusting for altitude if required. Once the timer goes off, turn off the burner.

7. Once you are done with the processing, let the pressure release naturally before opening the canner and taking out the jars. Let the jars cool completely on your countertop for no less than 12 hours. Wipe the jars with a dry kitchen cloth or paper towel. Make sure to check for the seals. These jars will last you for about 12 months.

8. **Serving suggestion**: Empty the contents of the jar into a pan and place the pan over high heat. Add cornstarch mixture and stir constantly until thick. Serve over hot cooked rice. Garnish with parsley and serve.

# Chicken Marsala

Makes: 20 pint jars (500 ml) or 10 quart jars (1 L)

**Ingredients:**

- 10-12 pounds (4.5-5 kg) boneless, skinless chicken, trimmed of fat, cut into bite size pieces

- 4 cups (1 L) dry Marsala wine

- Two medium onions, diced

- Two large cloves garlic, chopped

- Four packages (20 ounces (567 g) each) sliced mushrooms

- 4 quarts (4 L) chicken stock

- 1 teaspoon (1 g) dried oregano

- Salt to taste

- Pepper to taste

- Olive oil to cook chicken, as required

Serving instructions per 1 pint jar (500 ml):

- Chopped parsley

- 1 tablespoon (15 g) cornstarch mixed with ¼ cup (125 ml) water

- 4 tablespoons (60 ml) cream or sour cream

- Cooked angel hair pasta or rice to serve

**Directions:**

1. Arrange the pressure canner, canning lids, and jars. You need twenty 1 pint (500 ml) size jars or ten quart size (1 L) jars. Pour enough water into the pressure canner following the manufacturer's instructions such that it is about 3 inches (8 centimeters) in height from the bottom of the canner. Place the canner on your stovetop over low heat. Place the jars in the canner so that the jars remain warm. The temperature of the water in the canner should be maintained at 180°F (82°C). Place the lids in a small saucepan of water over low heat on another burner.

2. Pour oil into a large pan and let the oil heat over high heat. Sprinkle salt and pepper over the chicken and cook them in batches until brown on the outside. Place a colander over a bowl. Take out the chicken from the pan and place it in the colander so that excess fat will drain off.

3. Lift the jars from the canner and place over the towel. Divide the chicken equally and pack into the jars. Divide the mushrooms into the jars.

4. Add onion, and oregano into the pan in which you cooked the chicken and cook the onions until pink. Pour wine and let it come to a rolling boil for a minute. Lower the heat and let it cook for about 3-4 minutes.

5. Pour stock and stir. Once the mixture starts boiling, let it cook on low heat for five minutes. Place a funnel over the jars and pour the stock mixture into the jars covering the mixture. Leave headspace of 1 inch (2.5 cm).

6. Make sure to remove bubbles using a bubble removing tool. Reassess the headspace and add more liquid if required to fill up to the required headspace.

7. Take a clean damp cloth and wipe the rim of the jars. Place the canning lid on each jar using the lid lifter. Place the canning ring on each jar and tighten it as suggested.

8. Place the jars in the canner and process the jars following the manufacturer's instruction manual at 10 psi (69 kPa). Set the timer for 75 minutes, adjusting for altitude if required. Once the timer goes off, turn off the burner.

9. Once you are done with the processing, let the pressure release naturally before opening the canner and taking out the jars. Let the jars cool completely on your countertop for

no less than 12 hours. Wipe the jars with a dry kitchen cloth or paper towel. Make sure to check for the seals. These jars will last you for about 12 months.

10. **Serving suggestion**: Empty the contents of the jar into a pan and place the pan over high heat. Add cornstarch mixture and stir constantly until thick. Add sour cream or cream and stir. Turn off the heat. Serve rice or pasta in serving plates or bowls. Ladle the chicken Marsala on top of the rice or pasta and serve garnished with parsley.

# Apricot Chicken

Makes: 4 pint jars (500 ml) or 2 quart jars (1 L)

## Ingredients:

- 3 pounds (1.4 kg) chicken breast or chicken breast tenderloins

- ½ teaspoon (2.5 g) spice mix of your choice per pint size jar or 1 teaspoon (5 g) spice mix per quart size jar

- 2 packages dried apricots

- 2 cups (500 ml) chicken broth

Serving instructions per 1 pint jar (500 ml):

- Hot cooked rice or egg noodles

## Directions:

1. Arrange the pressure canner, canning lids, and jars. You need four 1 pint (500 ml) size jars or two quart size (1 L) jars. Pour enough water into the pressure canner following the manufacturer's instructions such that it is about 3 inches (8 centimeters) in height from the bottom of the canner. Place the canner on your stovetop over low heat. Place the jars in the canner so that the jars remain warm. The temperature of the water in the

canner should be maintained at 180°F (82°C). Place the lids in a small saucepan of water over low heat on another burner.

2. Boil broth in a pot.

3. Lift the jars from the canner and place over the towel. Drop 4-5 apricots into each jar. Add spice mix into each jar. Fill chicken up to half of each jar. Drop 2-3 apricots in the jar once again. Divide the remaining chicken among the jars. Place remaining apricots in the jar. Place a funnel over the jars and pour the broth into the jars. Leave headspace of 1 inch (2.5 cm).

4. Make sure to remove bubbles using a bubble removing tool. Reassess the headspace and add more liquid if required to fill up to the required headspace.

5. Take a clean damp cloth and wipe the rim of the jars. Place the canning lid on each jar using the lid lifter. Place the canning ring on each jar and tighten it as suggested.

6. Place the jars in the canner and process the jars following the manufacturer's instruction manual at 10 psi (69 kPa). Set the timer for 75 minutes, adjusting for altitude if required. Once the timer goes off, turn off the burner.

7. Once you are done with the processing, let the pressure release naturally before opening the canner and taking out the jars. Let the jars cool completely on your countertop for no less than 12 hours. Wipe the jars with a dry kitchen cloth or paper towel. Make sure to check for the seals. These jars will last you for about 12 months.

8. **Serving suggestion**: Empty the contents of the jar into a pan and place the pan over high heat and heat thoroughly. Serve apricot chicken over rice or egg noodles.

# White Bean and Chicken Chili

Makes: 6 pint jars (500 ml)

**Ingredients:**

- 1 ¼ cups Great Northern beans, soaked in water overnight

- 3 cups boneless, skinless chicken cubes

- Three cloves garlic, minced

- ½ tablespoon dried oregano

- 5 cups low-fat chicken broth

- ½ tablespoon olive oil

- ½ medium onion, chopped

- 1/8 teaspoon ground cumin

- ½ teaspoon cayenne pepper

- ½ cup diced green chilies

Serving instructions per serving 1 pint (500 ml) jar:

- Diced tomatoes

- Diced avocado

- Chopped cilantro

**Directions:**

1. Put the soaked beans along with the soaked water into a pot and cook it over medium-high heat for 30 minutes. Drain.

2. Arrange the pressure canner, canning lids, and jars. You need six 1 pint (500 ml) size jars. Pour enough water into the pressure canner following the manufacturer's instructions such that it is about 3 inches (8 centimeters) in height from the bottom of the canner. Place the canner on your stovetop over low heat. Place the jars in the canner so that the jars remain warm. The temperature of the water in the canner should be maintained at

180°F (82°C). Place the lids in a small saucepan of water over low heat on another burner.

3. Meanwhile, pour oil into another pot and place it over medium heat. Stir in the chicken. Stir often and cook for about 8–10 minutes.

4. Stir in garlic, onions, oregano, cumin, and cayenne pepper. Place the beans in the pot.

5. Stir in the green chilies and broth. When the mixture starts boiling, reduce the heat to medium-low and let it cook for 8–9 minutes. Turn off the heat.

6. Place the jars on a towel. Place the funnel over the rim of the jar. Remove beans and chicken with a slotted spoon and add into the jars, making sure each jar has equal amounts of beans and chicken. The jars would be about half filled with the vegetables and meat.

7. Now pour the broth into the jars until you get 1 inch (2.5 cm) headspace.

8. Make sure to remove bubbles using a bubble removing tool. Reassess the headspace and add more boiling liquid if required to fill up to the required headspace.

9. Take a clean damp cloth and wipe the rim of the jars. Place the canning lid on each jar using the lid lifter. Place the canning ring on each jar and tighten it as suggested.

10. Place the jars in the canner and process the jars following the manufacturer's instruction manual at 10 psi (69 kPa). Set the timer for 70 minutes for 1 pint size (500 ml) jars, adjusting for altitude if required. Once the timer goes off, turn off the burner.

11. Once you are done with the processing, let the pressure release naturally before opening the canner and taking out the jars. Let the jars cool completely on your countertop for no less than 12 hours. Wipe the jars with a dry kitchen cloth or paper towel. Make sure to check for the seals. These jars will last you for about 12 months.

12. **Serving suggestion**: Empty the contents of a jar into a saucepan. Place the saucepan over medium heat. Heat the chili thoroughly. Serve garnished with avocado, tomatoes and cilantro.

# Bourbon Chicken

Makes: 6 pint jars (500 ml)

**Ingredients:**

- 4 pounds chicken, cut into bite size pieces

- Two cloves garlic, crushed

- ½ cup apple juice

- 4 tablespoons ketchup

- 1 cup water

- 4 tablespoons oil

- 2 teaspoons crushed red pepper

- 2/3 cup light brown sugar

- 2 tablespoons cider vinegar

- 2/3 cup soy sauce

Serving instructions per serving 1 pint (500 ml) jar:

- Sliced green onion

- 1 teaspoon cornstarch mixed with 2 tablespoons water (optional)

**Directions:**

1. Arrange the pressure canner, canning lids, and jars. You need six 1 pint (500 ml) size jars. Pour enough water into the pressure canner following the manufacturer's instructions such that it is about 3 inches (8 centimeters) in height from the bottom of the canner. Place the canner on your stovetop over low heat. Place the jars in the canner so that the jars remain warm. The temperature of the water in the canner should be maintained at

180°F (82°C). Place the lids in a small saucepan of water over low heat on another burner.

2. Combine garlic, apple juice, ketchup, water, red pepper, sugar, vinegar, and soy sauce in a saucepan and let it come to a boil. Stir occasionally. Turn off the heat.

3. Meanwhile, heat oil in another pan and add chicken. Cook until the chicken is light brown. Turn off the heat.

4. Place the jars on a towel. Place the funnel over the rim of the jar. Divide the chicken and sauce among the jars, leaving a headspace of 1 inch (2.5 cm).

5. If you do not have this headspace, pour some apple juice or water to get the headspace.

6. Make sure to remove bubbles using a bubble removing tool. Reassess the headspace and add more boiling liquid if required to fill up to the required headspace.

7. Take a clean damp cloth and wipe the rim of the jars. Place the canning lid on each jar using the lid lifter. Place the canning ring on each jar and tighten it as suggested.

8. Place the jars in the canner and process the jars following the manufacturer's instruction manual at 10 psi (69 kPa). Set the timer for 75 minutes for 1 pint size (500 ml) jars, adjusting for altitude if required. Once the timer goes off, turn off the burner.

9. Once you are done with the processing, let the pressure release naturally before opening the canner and taking out the jars. Let the jars cool completely on your countertop for no less than 12 hours. Wipe the jars with a dry kitchen cloth or paper towel. Make sure to check for the seals. These jars will last you for about 12 months.

10. **Serving suggestion**: Empty the contents of a jar into a saucepan. Place the saucepan over medium heat. Heat thoroughly and serve. If the sauce is watery, stir in cornstarch mixture and stir constantly until thick.

# Sweet and Sour Chicken

Makes: 10 quart jars (1 L)

**Ingredients:**

- 5 pounds cooked chicken, cut into cubes or shredded

- Four medium onions, cut into large dice

- Four green bell pepper, deseeded, cut into 1 inch (2.5 cm) squares

- Two red bell peppers, deseeded, cut into 1 inch (2.4 cm) squares

- Six cans {15 ounces (425 g) each} pineapple chunks

- 3 cups (639 g) packed brown sugar

- 6 cups (1.5 L) pineapple juice

- 5 cups (1.25 L) white vinegar

- 1 cup (250 ml) ketchup

- 1 ½ cups (357 ml) soy sauce

- 2 inches (5 cm) fresh ginger, peeled, grated

Serving instructions per 1 pint jar (500 ml): Use any one or two of these

- Hot cooked rice or egg noodles

- Chinese potato salad

- Cucumber salad

- Vegetables tossed in noodles

- Broccoli and garlic stir-fry

- Egg fried rice

## Directions:

1. Arrange the pressure canner, canning lids, and jars. You need ten quart size (1 L) jars. Pour enough water into the pressure canner following the manufacturer's instructions such that it is about 3 inches (8 centimeters) in height from the bottom of the canner. Place the canner on your stovetop over low heat. Place the jars in the canner so that the jars remain warm. The temperature of the water in the canner should be maintained at 180°F (82°C). Place the lids in a small saucepan of water over low heat on another burner.

2. Lift the jars from the canner and place over the towel. Open the cans of pineapple. Place a colander over a large bowl and drain the pineapple into the colander. We need the drained pineapple juice as well as the pineapple juice that is mentioned in the ingredients section.

3. You now have to place the ingredients in layers in the jars. Start off layering the jars with chicken followed by onions. Next place bell peppers in the jars followed by pineapple. Make sure you distribute the chicken, onions, bell peppers, and pineapple chunks in the jars.

4. Combine brown sugar, soy sauce, vinegar, pineapple juice and 6 cups of the retained pineapple juice into a large saucepan. Place the saucepan over medium heat and stir often until sugar dissolves completely. When the sauce mixture begins to boil, turn off the heat.

5. Place a funnel over the jars and pour the sauce mixture into the jars. Leave headspace of 1 inch (2.5 cm).

6. Make sure to remove bubbles using a bubble removing tool. Reassess the headspace and add more liquid if required to fill up to the required headspace.

7. Take a clean damp cloth and wipe the rim of the jars. Place the canning lid on each jar using the lid lifter. Place the canning ring on each jar and tighten it as suggested.

8. Place the jars in the canner and process the jars following the manufacturer's instruction manual at 10 psi (69 kPa). Set the timer for 90 minutes, adjusting for altitude if required. Once the timer goes off, turn off the burner.

9. Once you are done with the processing, let the pressure release naturally before opening the canner and taking out the jars. Let the jars cool completely on your countertop for no less than 12 hours. Wipe the jars with a dry kitchen cloth or paper towel. Make sure to check for the seals. These jars will last you for about 12 months.

10. **Serving suggestion**: Empty the contents of the jar into a pan and place the pan over high heat and heat thoroughly. Serve with any one of the suggested serving options.

# Venison Stew

Makes: 14 quart jars (1 L)

**Ingredients:**

- 14 cups (2.1 kg) cubed venison stew meat

- Eight medium carrots, peeled, diced (around 8 cups after dicing)

- Eight stalks celery, chopped

- 20 cups (5 L) beef broth or more if required

- Eight large onions, chopped (about 8 cups after dicing)

- Eight medium potatoes, peeled, diced (about 8 cups after dicing)

- ½ cup seasoning blend of your choice

Serving instructions per 1 quart jar (1 L):
- Hot cooked rice or noodles

- Side dish of your choice

- 1 tablespoon (15 g) cornstarch mixed with 2 tablespoons water

**Directions:**

1. First of all arrange the pressure canner, canning lids, and jars. You need fourteen quart size (1 L) jars. Pour enough water into the pressure canner following the manufacturer's instructions such that it is about 3 inches (8 centimeters) in height from the bottom of the canner. Place the canner on your stovetop over low heat. Place the jars in the canner so that the jars remain warm. The temperature of the water in the canner should be maintained at 180°F (82°C). Place the lids in a small saucepan of water over low heat on another burner.

2. Boil broth in a pot.

3. Meanwhile, combine meat in a large bowl with seasoning blend. Place a cup of the meat in each jar. Layer with ½ cup of each vegetable over the meat in any manner you please. Make it look colorful and appealing.

4. Place a funnel over the jars and pour boiling broth into the jars. Leave headspace of 1 inch (2.5 cm).

5. Make sure to remove bubbles using a bubble removing tool. Reassess the headspace and add more liquid if required to fill up to the required headspace.

6. Take a clean damp cloth and wipe the rim of the jars. Place the canning lid on each jar using the lid lifter. Place the canning ring on each jar and tighten it as suggested.

7. Place the jars in the canner and process the jars following the manufacturer's instruction manual at 10 psi (69 kPa). Set the timer for 90 minutes, adjusting for altitude if required. Once the timer goes off, turn off the burner.

8. Once you are done with the processing, let the pressure release naturally before opening the canner and taking out the jars. Let the jars cool completely on your countertop for no less than 12 hours. Wipe the jars with a dry kitchen cloth or paper towel. Make sure to check for the seals. These jars will last you for about 12 months.

9. **Serving suggestion**: Empty the contents of the jar into a pan and place the pan over high heat. Stir in the cornstarch mixture and heat thoroughly, stirring constantly until thick. Serve with a side dish of your choice. If you do not have any particular favorites, I suggest a few side dishes like homemade regular bread or garlic bread, mashed potatoes, green salad, cheddar cheese biscuits, cooked rice, rice pilaf, etc.

# Venison Spaghetti Sauce

Makes: 14 quart jars (1 L)

## Ingredients:

- ½ cup (125 ml) olive oil

- Two large yellow onions, minced

- Two cans (6 ounces each) tomato paste

- ¼ cup (12 g) dried oregano

- 1 teaspoon (5 g) red pepper flakes

- 2 quarts (2 L) venison stock or beef stock

- Two cans {28 ounces (794 g) each} crushed tomatoes

- Salt to taste

- Sugar to taste

- Pepper to taste

- 5 pounds (2.27 kg) ground venison

- 12 cloves garlic, peeled, minced

- 2 cups (500 ml) red wine

- ½ cup (30.8 g) minced fresh parsley

Serving instructions per 1 quart jar (1 L):

- Hot cooked spaghetti or any other pasta

**Directions:**

1. Not just venison, you can make this sauce with any kind of ground meat. So you can change ground venison meat to any other meat of your choice.

2. Add venison into a large Dutch oven or a large heavy pot and place the pot over medium-high heat. If your meat has come with all fat removed from it, only then you need to add all of the olive oil to cook the meat. But if the meat has a little fat, you need to add only a little of the olive oil. You decide on how much oil is to be added.

3. Cook until the meat is brown. As you stir, break the meat into crumbles. Now add onions and cook until onions are soft. Make sure to stir the mixture frequently. Add

garlic and cook for a couple of minutes. Next goes in the tomato paste. Stir until well combined. Cook for about 2-3 minutes, making sure to stir often.

4.  Add wine, oregano, red pepper flakes, and parsley and stir until well combined. Cook until the wine is half its original quantity. Stir in the stock and tomatoes and let it come to a boil. Now reduce the heat and cook for about 45 minutes. Stir in sugar, salt, and pepper.

5.  Once you add the tomatoes into the pot and reduce the heat, it is time for you to arrange the pressure canner, canning lids, and jars. You need fourteen quart size (1 L) jars. Pour enough water into the pressure canner following the manufacturer's instructions such that it is about 3 inches (8 centimeters) in height from the bottom of the canner. Place the canner on your stovetop over low heat. Place the jars in the canner so that the jars remain warm. The temperature of the water in the canner should be maintained at 180°F (82°C). Place the lids in a small saucepan of water over low heat on another burner.

6.  Place the jars over a towel. Place a funnel over the jars and pour the sauce mixture into the jars. Leave headspace of 1 inch (2.5 cm).

7.  Make sure to remove bubbles using a bubble removing tool. Reassess the headspace and add more liquid if required to fill up to the required headspace.

8.  Take a clean damp cloth and wipe the rim of the jars. Place the canning lid on each jar using the lid lifter. Place the canning ring on each jar and tighten it as suggested.

9.  Place the jars in the canner and process the jars following the manufacturer's instruction manual at 10 psi (69 kPa). Set the timer for 70 minutes, adjusting for altitude if required. Once the timer goes off, turn off the burner.

10. Once you are done with the processing, let the pressure release naturally before opening the canner and taking out the jars. Let the jars cool completely on your countertop for no less than 12 hours. Wipe the jars with a dry kitchen cloth or paper towel. Make sure to check for the seals. These jars will last you for about 24 months.

11. **Serving suggestion**: Empty the contents of the jar into a pan and place the pan over medium heat and heat thoroughly. Add pasta and toss well. Serve right away with some cheese if you wish. There are numerous ways you can use the spaghetti sauce. You can

use it to make lasagna, shepherd's pie, top it over hot dogs and nachos, fill it up in bell peppers, spread it over crepes, fajitas etc.

# Spicy Turkey Burgers

Makes: 3 quart jars (1 L)

**Ingredients:**

- 4 pounds (1.8 kg) lean ground turkey

- 2 inches (5 cm) fresh ginger root, peeled, minced

- Two medium onions, diced

- 2 teaspoons (10 g) salt

- 2 tablespoons (30 g) freshly ground black pepper

- 2 tablespoons (30 g) ground dry mustard

- 1 tablespoon (15 ml) Worcestershire sauce

- Eight large cloves garlic, minced

- 4 fresh green chili peppers, minced

- ½ cup (30.8 g) finely chopped cilantro

- ½ cup (125 ml) low-sodium soy sauce

- 6 tablespoons (40.8 g) paprika

- 2 tablespoons (30 g) ground cumin

- Boiling water or stock or tomato juice as required

<u>Serving instructions per burger:</u>

- One burger bun

- One lettuce leaf

- One cheese slice (optional)

- Any other toppings of your choice

**Directions:**

1. Combine turkey meat, onion, chili pepper, Worcestershire sauce, soy sauce, paprika, cilantro, ginger, garlic, pepper, mustard, cumin, and salt in a large bowl. Make sure you do not use any binders like eggs or breadcrumbs.

2. Make patties of the meat mixture such that they are as wide as the mouth of the jar and they fit well into the jars. You can use your hands to shape the patties. You can also use the help of the canning rings to shape the burgers. You should use a wide mouth jar to can the burgers. You can cook the patties in a pan or in an oven. They only need to be browned and not cooked through inside. Boil water, stock or tomato juice in a pot.

3. To cook them in the oven, place the patties on a baking sheet and bake them in an oven that has been preheated to 375°F for about 15 minutes on each side.

4. If you are cooking them in batches, make sure the burgers are kept warm until you place them in the jars.

5. While the burgers are cooking, arrange the pressure canner, canning lids, and jars. You need about three quart (1L) size jars. Pour enough water into the pressure canner following the manufacturer's instructions such that it is about 3 inches (8 centimeters) in height from the bottom of the canner. Place the canner on your stovetop over low heat. Place the jars in the canner so that the jars remain warm. The temperature of the water in the canner should be maintained at 180°F (82°C). Place the lids in a small saucepan of water over low heat on another burner.

6. Place a kitchen towel on your countertop and spread it. Lift the jars from the canner and place over the towel. Place the burgers in the jars. Pour the chosen boiling liquid into the jars to cover the burgers leaving headspace of 1 inch (2.5 cm).

7. Make sure to remove bubbles using a bubble removing tool. Reassess the headspace and add more liquid if required to fill up to the required headspace.

8. Take a clean damp cloth and wipe the rim of the jars. Place the canning lid on each jar using the lid lifter. Place the canning ring on each jar and tighten it as suggested.

9. Place the jars in the canner and process the jars following the manufacturer's instruction manual at 10 psi (69 kPa). Set the timer for 90 minutes, adjusting for altitude if required. Once the timer goes off, turn off the burner.

10. Once you are done with the processing, let the pressure release naturally before opening the canner and taking out the jars. Let the jars cool completely on your countertop for no less than 12 hours. Wipe the jars with a dry kitchen cloth or paper towel. Make sure to check for the seals. These jars will last you for about 12 months.

11. **Serving instructions**: Take out a burger from the jar and place on a hot pan over medium heat. You can spray some oil into the pan before placing the burger and cook until crisp on both the sides. Split the bun into 2 and lightly toast the bun. Place a lettuce leaf over the bottom half of the bun followed by the burger and a slice of cheese. Place any other topping or sauce of your choice. Cover with the top half of the bun and serve. Make sure to keep the opened jar in the refrigerator and use it as soon as possible.

# Turkey and Gravy

Makes: 8 quart jars (1 L)

**Ingredients:**

- 4 cups (700 g) chopped onion

- 4 cups (500 g) finely chopped celery

- 6 cups (1,050 g) peeled, diced potatoes

- 8 pounds (3.6 kg) boneless turkey cut into 2 inch (5 cm) chunks

- 1 teaspoon (5 g) salt per quart (1 L) size jar

- 1 teaspoon (5 g) poultry seasoning per quart (1 L) size jar

- ½ teaspoon (2.5 g) ground black pepper per quart (1 L) size jar

- 2 tablespoons (30 ml) dry white wine per quart (1 L) size jar (optional)

- Boiling turkey broth or water, as required

Serving instructions per 1 pint jar (500 ml):

- Chopped parsley

- 1 tablespoon (15 g) flour

- Hot cooked rice

**Directions:**

1. Arrange the pressure canner, canning lids, and jars. You need eight quart size (1 L) jars. Pour enough water into the pressure canner following the manufacturer's instructions such that it is about 3 inches (8 centimeters) in height from the bottom of the canner. Place the canner on your stovetop over low heat. Place the jars in the canner so that the jars remain warm. The temperature of the water in the canner should be maintained at

180°F (82°C). Place the lids in a small saucepan of water over low heat on another burner.

2. Boil a pot of water or broth.

3. Place a kitchen towel on your countertop and spread it. Lift the jars from the canner and place over the towel. Add salt, poultry seasoning, pepper and dry white wine if using, into each jar. Divide the meat into the jars. Next layer with ½ cup celery in each jar followed by ½ cup onions. Finally divide the potatoes among the jars. Pour boiling liquid into the jars to cover the mixture leaving a headspace of 1 inch (2.5 cm).

4. Make sure to remove bubbles using a bubble removing tool. Reassess the headspace and add more liquid if required to fill up to the required headspace.

5. Take a clean damp cloth and wipe the rim of the jars. Place the canning lid on each jar using the lid lifter. Place the canning ring on each jar and tighten it as suggested.

6. Place the jars in the canner and process the jars following the manufacturer's instruction manual at 10 psi (69 kPa). Set the timer for 75 minutes, adjusting for altitude if required. Once the timer goes off, turn off the burner.

7. Once you are done with the processing, let the pressure release naturally before opening the canner and taking out the jars. Let the jars cool completely on your countertop for no less than 12 hours. Wipe the jars with a dry kitchen cloth or paper towel. Make sure to check for the seals. These jars will last you for about 12 months.

8. **Serving suggestion**: Empty the contents of the jar into a pan and place the pan over high heat. Add flour into a bowl. Add a little of the liquid (before it gets hot) from the can into the bowl and stir well. Add the mixture and stir constantly until thick. Serve over hot cooked rice. Garnish with parsley and serve.

# Asian Turkey Meatballs

Makes: 5 pint jars (500 ml)

## Ingredients:

- 1 ½ pounds (680g) lean ground turkey

- 1 inch (2.5 cm) fresh ginger, peeled, grated

- ½ teaspoon (2.5 g) garlic powder

- ½ teaspoon (2.5 g) freshly ground pepper

- 1 tablespoon (15 ml) soy sauce

- Two green onions, finely chopped

- Three cloves garlic, peeled, grated

- 1 ½ teaspoons (7.5 g) salt

- 2 ½ tablespoons (37.5 ml) teriyaki ginger sauce

- Red pepper flakes to taste (optional)

- Boiling chicken stock, as required

Serving instructions per serving 1 pint (500 ml) jar:
- Hot cooked egg noodles or rice

Sauce to serve:
- 4 tablespoons (60 ml) light soy sauce

- 2 teaspoons (10 ml) honey

- ½ inch (1.25 cm) fresh ginger, minced

- ½ teaspoon (2.5 ml) sesame oil

- 1 tablespoon (15 g) cornstarch

- Hot sauce to taste

- Two cloves garlic, minced

**Directions:**

1. Combine turkey, salt, ginger, soy sauce, teriyaki sauce, green onion, garlic, and spices in a bowl. Make 30 equal portions of the mixture and shape them into small balls. The balls may be about 1.5 inches (3.75 cm) each. I suggest you dip your hands often in water and make the meatballs. This way the meat will not stick to your hands. Make sure you do not add any binders like egg or breadcrumbs.

2. Next thing to be done is to arrange the pressure canner, canning lids, and jars. You need about five 1 pint (500 ml) size jars. Pour enough water into the pressure canner following the manufacturer's instructions such that it is about 3 inches (8 centimeters) in height from the bottom of the canner. Place the canner on your stovetop over low heat. Place the jars in the canner so that the jars remain warm. The temperature of the water in the canner should be maintained at 180°F (82°C). Place the lids in a small saucepan of water over low heat on another burner.

3. Boil chicken stock in a pot.

4. Place a skillet over medium heat. Spray some cooking spray into the skillet. Add a few meatballs into the pan without overcrowding. And cook until brown all over, turning the meatballs occasionally. It should not be cooked through as it will be cooked further while processing. Remove the meatballs from the pan and make sure to keep them warm until the remaining meatballs are browned. You can also bake the meatballs in an oven for about 45 minutes in a preheated oven at a temperature of 350°F. Turn the meatballs every 15 minutes in the oven.

5. Place the jars over a towel on your countertop. Place six meatballs in each jar. Pour enough boiling stock into the jars until you get headspace of 1 inch (2.5 cm)

6. Make sure to remove bubbles using a bubble removing tool. Reassess the headspace and add more boiling liquid if required to fill up to the required headspace.

7. Take a clean damp cloth and wipe the rim of the jars. Place the canning lid on each jar using the lid lifter. Place the canning ring on each jar and tighten it as suggested.

8. Place the jars in the canner and process the jars following the manufacturer's instruction manual at 10 psi (69 kPa). Set the timer for 75 minutes for a pint (500 ml) size jar, adjusting for altitude if required. Once the timer goes off, turn off the burner.

9. Once you are done with the processing, let the pressure release naturally before opening the canner and taking out the jars. Let the jars cool completely on your countertop for no less than 12 hours. Wipe the jars with a dry kitchen cloth or paper towel. Make sure to check for the seals. These jars will last you for about 12 months.

10. **Serving suggestion**: Empty the broth from the jar into a saucepan. Take out some liquid from the jar and add it into a bowl. Add the sauce ingredients into the bowl and whisk well. Place the saucepan over medium heat. Pour the sauce mixture into the saucepan and keep stirring until the sauce thickens. Add meatballs and stir until the meatballs are well coated with the sauce. Let the meatballs heat through. Serve over egg noodles or hot cooked rice.

# Chapter 6:
# Vegetables

## Green Beans

Makes: 16 pint jars (500 ml)

**Ingredients:**

- 10 pounds (4.8 kg) green beans, trimmed (make sure they are fresh and tender)

- Boiling water, as required

- ½ teaspoon (2.5 g) salt per pint size jar (optional)

- 10 large cloves garlic, peeled

Serving instructions per serving 1 pint (500 ml) jar:

- One onion, thinly sliced

- Salt and pepper to taste

- Red pepper flakes to taste

- Any spices of your choice to taste

- Oil to cook, as required

**Directions:**

1. Firstly arrange the pressure canner, canning lids, and jars. You need about sixteen 1 pint (500 ml) size jars. Pour enough water into the pressure canner following the manufacturer's instructions such that it is about 3 inches (8 centimeters) in height from

the bottom of the canner. Place the canner on your stovetop over low heat. Place the jars in the canner so that the jars remain warm. The temperature of the water in the canner should be maintained at 180°F (82°C). Place the lids in a small saucepan of water over low heat on another burner.

2. Meanwhile, wash the green beans well. Cut the beans into pieces of about 2 inches or as per your choice.

3. Place a clove of garlic in each jar. Sprinkle salt in each jar if using.

4. Meanwhile, boil a pot of water to fill the jars and another pot of water if you want to cook the green beans.

5. If you want to can the green beans raw, simply fill it into the canning jars. Make sure you pack them tightly. If you want to can cooked green beans, drop them in one of the pots of boiling water and cook for five minutes. Drain the green beans in a colander. Pack the cooked beans lightly in the jars.

6. Place a kitchen towel on your countertop and spread it. Lift the jars from the canner and place over the towel.

7. Place the funnel on the rim of the jar and pour boiling water from the other pot into the jar to cover the green beans leaving headspace of 1 inch (2.5 cm).

8. Make sure to remove bubbles using a bubble removing tool. Reassess the headspace and add more boiling liquid if required to fill up to the required headspace.

9. Take a clean damp cloth and wipe the rim of the jars. Place the canning lid on each jar using the lid lifter. Place the canning ring on each jar and tighten it as suggested.

10. Place the jars in the canner and process the jars following the manufacturer's instruction manual at 10 psi (69 kPa). Set the timer for 20 minutes for a pint (500 ml) size jar, adjusting for altitude if required. Once the timer goes off, turn off the burner.

11. Once you are done with the processing, let the pressure release naturally before opening the canner and taking out the jars. Let the jars cool completely on your countertop for

no less than 12 hours. Wipe the jars with a dry kitchen cloth or paper towel. Make sure to check for the seals. These jars will last you for about 12 months.

12. **Serving suggestion**: Drain the contents of the jar into a colander. Place a pan over high heat. Add a splash of oil and let the oil heat. Add onion slices and cook until translucent. Add the green beans, salt, pepper, red pepper flakes and any other spices of your choice and mix well. Heat thoroughly and serve.

# Ratatouille

Makes: 10 – 11 pint jars (500 ml)

**Ingredients:**

- 10 tablespoons (150 ml) extra-virgin olive oil, divided
- 2 pounds (907 g) zucchini or summer squash, discard stems and cut into 1 inch cubes
- Six large whole tomatoes
- Eight cloves garlic, peeled, minced
- 2 teaspoons (2.3 g) minced fresh thyme leaves
- Freshly ground black pepper to taste
- 2 pounds (907 g) eggplant, cut into 1 inch chunks
- Six medium onions, cut into thick slices
- Four large red bell peppers, cut into 1 inch (2.5 cm) squares
- ½ cup (27.2 g) torn fresh basil leaves
- Salt to taste

Serving instructions per serving 1 pint (500 ml) jar:

- Chopped fresh basil and thyme

**Directions:**

1. Set up your oven to broil mode and preheat it to high heat.

2. Place eggplants, onion, zucchini, onion, and bell pepper in a large bowl. Drizzle 8 tablespoons of oil over the vegetables and toss them up well. The vegetables should be coated in oil.

3. Take two large baking sheets and line them with parchment paper. Scatter the vegetables on the baking sheets, spreading it evenly. Place the tomatoes in between the vegetables and place the baking sheets in the oven in batches and broil for a few minutes until

visibly brown at a few places. Make doubly sure they do not burn. Take out the tomatoes from the baking sheet and keep them aside on a plate. These will be used later.

4. Arrange the pressure canner, canning lids, and jars. You need about ten to eleven pint (500 ml) size jars. Pour enough water into the pressure canner following the manufacturer's instructions such that it is about 3 inches (8 centimeters) in height from the bottom of the canner. Place the canner on your stovetop over low heat. Place the jars in the canner so that the jars remain warm. The temperature of the water in the canner should be maintained at 180°F (82°C). Place the lids in a small saucepan of water over low heat on another burner.

5. Pour 2 tablespoons (30 ml) oil into a large pot and place the pot over medium-low heat.

6. Add garlic and cook for a few seconds until you get a nice aroma in the air. Stir in thyme. Add the broiled vegetables from the baking sheet and mix well. Let the vegetables cook for about five minutes. Stir occasionally.

7. Meanwhile, take out the stems and peel from the tomatoes. Try to take out the seed part as well and keep the pulp on your cutting board. Chop pulp into coarse pieces and add into the pot along with vegetables. Mix well and turn off the heat. Add basil, pepper, and salt and mix well.

8. Place a kitchen towel on your countertop and spread it. Lift the jars from the canner and place over the towel.

9. Pack the hot vegetables into the jars leaving headspace of 1 ½ inches (3.75 cm). Make sure to remove bubbles using a bubble removing tool. Reassess the headspace and add more vegetables if required to fill up to the required headspace.

10. Take a clean damp cloth and wipe the rim of the jars. Place the canning lid on each jar using the lid lifter. Place the canning ring on each jar and tighten it as suggested.

11. Place the jars in the canner and process the jars following the manufacturer's instruction manual at 10 psi (69 kPa). Set the timer for 30 minutes for a pint (500 ml) size jar, adjusting for altitude if required. The time for altitudes 1,001 to 6,000 feet is 20 minutes though and beyond 6,001 feet is 25 minutes. Once the timer goes off, turn off the burner.

12. Once you are done with the processing, let the pressure release naturally before opening the canner and taking out the jars. Let the jars cool completely on your countertop for no less than 12 hours. Wipe the jars with a dry kitchen cloth or paper towel. Make sure to check for the seals. These jars will last you for about 12 months.

13. **Serving suggestion**: Empty the contents of a jar into a pan. Heat thoroughly and serve garnished with basil and thyme.

# Herbed Potatoes

Makes: 8 pint jars (500 ml) or 4 quart jars (1 L)

**Ingredients:**

- 5 pounds (2.3 kg) white potatoes, halved or quartered, depending on the size but no more than 2 inches (5 cm)

- Boiling chicken broth or vegetable broth or water as required

- 4 teaspoons (20 g) salt

- 2 teaspoons (2 g) dried rosemary

- 2 teaspoon (10 g) ground black pepper

- 2 teaspoons (2 g) dried thyme

Serving instructions per serving 1 pint (500 ml) jar or quart (1 L) jar:
- Blob of butter

- Milk

## Directions:

1. As you start chopping potatoes, add them to a pot of cold water. This way some starch will be released from the potatoes also it will prevent the potatoes from browning.

2. Arrange the pressure canner, canning lids, and jars. You need eight 1 pint (500 ml) size jars or four quart size (1 L) jars. Pour enough water into the pressure canner following the manufacturer's instructions such that it is about 3 inches (8 centimeters) in height from the bottom of the canner. Place the canner on your stovetop over low heat. Place the jars in the canner so that the jars remain warm. The temperature of the water in the canner should be maintained at 180°F (82°C). Place the lids in a small saucepan of water over low heat on another burner.

3. Boil broth in a pot.

4. Lift the jars from the canner and place over the towel. Combine salt, oregano, thyme, and pepper in a bowl. Divide equally the spices among the jars. Pack the potatoes into the jars leaving headspace of 1 inch (2.5 cm). Pour boiling liquid into the jars to get the required headspace.

5.  Make sure to remove bubbles using a bubble removing tool. Reassess the headspace and add more boiling liquid if required to fill up to the required headspace.

6.  Take a clean damp cloth and wipe the rim of the jars. Place the canning lid on each jar using the lid lifter. Place the canning ring on each jar and tighten it as suggested.

7.  Place the jars in the canner and process the jars following the manufacturer's instruction manual at 10 psi (69 kPa). Set the timer for 35 minutes for a pint (500 ml) size jar or 40 minutes for quart (1L) size jars, adjusting for altitude if required. Once the timer goes off, turn off the burner.

8.  Once you are done with the processing, let the pressure release naturally before opening the canner and taking out the jars. Let the jars cool completely on your countertop for no less than 12 hours. Wipe the jars with a dry kitchen cloth or paper towel. Make sure to check for the seals. These jars will last you for about 12 months.

9.  **Serving instructions**: Empty the contents of a jar into a pan. Heat thoroughly. Drain off the liquid and transfer the potatoes into a bowl. Mash them adding some butter and milk. Add salt and pepper to taste and you now have mashed potatoes. You can add some fresh herbs as well. You can also use the drained potatoes in many ways like in salads, stir-fry the potatoes in oil with some spices if desired, etc.

# Roasted Root Vegetables

Makes: 12 pint jars (500 ml) or 6 quart jars (1 L)

**Ingredients:**

- 2 pounds (907 g) large beets, cut into 1 inch chunks

- 2 pounds (907 g) parsnips cut into 1 inch chunks

- 2 pounds (907 g) turnips cut into 1 inch chunks

- Four medium carrots, peeled**Error! Bookmark not defined.**, cut into 1 inch pieces

- 16 cups (4 L) chicken broth

- 1 cup (250 ml) orange juice

- 2 teaspoons (10 g) salt

- ½ cup (125 ml) olive oil

- 2 teaspoons (10 g) finely shredded orange peel

- 2 tablespoons (30 ml) bottled lemon juice

- 1 teaspoon (5 g) freshly ground black pepper

- 16 cups (4 L) chicken broth

- 1 cup (250 ml) orange juice

- 2 teaspoons (10 g) salt

Serving instructions per 1 quart jar (1 L):

- Grated parmesan cheese

- Two cloves garlic, minced

- A dash of oil

- Salt and pepper to taste

**Directions:**

1. Set up your oven and preheat it to 425°F. Place beets, parsnips, turnips and carrots in a bowl and toss well. Drizzle oil over the vegetables and toss well. Take two large baking sheets and line them with parchment paper. Scatter the vegetables on the baking sheets, spreading it evenly. Place the baking sheets in the oven together in the oven on 2 racks and bake for about 20 to 25 minutes. Make sure to exchange the baking sheets to ensure even cooking. The vegetables should be tender and brown at the edges.

2.  While the vegetables are roasting, arrange the pressure canner, canning lids, and jars. You need twelve 1 pint (500 ml) size jars or six quart size (1 L) jars. Pour enough water into the pressure canner following the manufacturer's instructions such that it is about 3 inches (8 centimeters) in height from the bottom of the canner. Place the canner on your stovetop over low heat. Place the jars in the canner so that the jars remain warm. The temperature of the water in the canner should be maintained at 180°F (82°C). Place the lids in a small saucepan of water over low heat on another burner.

3.  Boil broth, orange juice, orange peel, salt, pepper, and lemon juice in a pot. Place the jars on a towel. Distribute the vegetables among the jars. Pour boiling liquid into the jars to get the required headspace.

4.  Make sure to remove bubbles using a bubble removing tool. Reassess the headspace and add more boiling liquid if required to fill up to the required headspace.

5.  Take a clean damp cloth and wipe the rim of the jars. Place the canning lid on each jar using the lid lifter. Place the canning ring on each jar and tighten it as suggested.

6.  Place the jars in the canner and process the jars following the manufacturer's instruction manual at 10 psi (69 kPa). Set the timer for 75 minutes for quart (1L) size jars, adjusting for altitude if required. Once the timer goes off, turn off the burner.

7.  Once you are done with the processing, let the pressure release naturally before opening the canner and taking out the jars. Let the jars cool completely on your countertop for no less than 12 hours. Wipe the jars with a dry kitchen cloth or paper towel. Make sure to check for the seals. These jars will last you for about 12 months.

8.  **Serving suggestion**: You can make soup of the vegetables. For this, empty the contents of the jar into a blender and blend until smooth. Add salt and pepper to taste. Pour into a saucepan. Heat thoroughly and serve with grated cheese. To serve it as a side dish, drain off the liquid from the can. Pour oil into a pan and let it heat over high heat. Add garlic and cook for a few seconds until you get a nice aroma. Add roasted vegetables and stir-fry for a few minutes, until thoroughly heated. Add salt and pepper to taste. Transfer into a bowl. Garnish with cheese and serve.

# Chapter 7: Bonus Chapter -
# Soups

## Sweet Potato Soup

Makes: 8 pint jars (500 ml) or 4 quart jars (1 L)

**Ingredients:**

- Four large sweet potatoes, peeled, rinsed, cut into cubes

- 1 teaspoon (5 g) salt

- Two carrots, chopped

- Four cloves garlic, minced

- Ground pepper to taste

- 4 tablespoons oil

- 2 tablespoons red wine vinegar

- Two small onions, chopped

- Two stalks celery, chopped

- 2 teaspoons (5 g) chopped fresh rosemary

- 12 cups (1.5 L) chicken broth

<u>Serving instructions per serving 1 pint (500 ml) jar or quart (1 L) jar:</u>

- Grated cheese

- Chopped parsley

**Directions:**

1. Place sweet potatoes in a bowl. Add half of each-the oil, garlic, salt, and rosemary and toss well. Drizzle vinegar and toss well. Transfer the mixture onto a baking sheet and roast the sweet potatoes in a preheated oven at 450°F for 20 minutes.

2. Next arrange the pressure canner, canning lids, and jars. You need eight 1 pint (500 ml) size jars or four quart size (1 L) jars. Pour enough water into the pressure canner following the manufacturer's instructions such that it is about 3 inches (8 centimeters) in height from the bottom of the canner. Place the canner on your stovetop over low heat. Place the jars in the canner so that the jars remain warm. The temperature of the water in the canner should be maintained at 180°F (82°C). Place the lids in a small saucepan of water over low heat on another burner.

3. While the sweet potatoes are roasting, pour remaining oil into a stock pot. Place the stock pot over medium-high heat. Add onion, garlic, carrot, rosemary, and pepper and sauté for 4-5 minutes. Pour broth and let it come to a boil. Add salt and stir. Turn off the heat.

4. Place the jars on a towel. Distribute the sweet potatoes among the jars. Remove the vegetables from the stock pot with a slotted spoon and distribute them among the jars. Pour boiling broth into the jars to get 1 inch (2.5 cm) headspace.

5. Make sure to remove bubbles using a bubble removing tool. Reassess the headspace and add more boiling liquid if required to fill up to the required headspace.

6. Take a clean damp cloth and wipe the rim of the jars. Place the canning lid on each jar using the lid lifter. Place the canning ring on each jar and tighten it as suggested.

7. Place the jars in the canner and process the jars following the manufacturer's instruction manual at 10 psi (69 kPa). Set the timer for 60 minutes for 1 pint size (500 ml) jars or 75

minutes for quart (1L) size jars, adjusting for altitude if required. Once the timer goes off, turn off the burner.

8. Once you are done with the processing, let the pressure release naturally before opening the canner and taking out the jars. Let the jars cool completely on your countertop for no less than 12 hours. Wipe the jars with a dry kitchen cloth or paper towel. Make sure to check for the seals. These jars will last you for about 12 months.

9. **Serving suggestion**: Empty the contents of a can into a blender and blend until smooth. Pour the soup into a saucepan and heat thoroughly. Ladle into soup bowls and serve with cheese and parsley.

# Carrot and Fennel Soup

Makes: 6 pint jars (500 ml) or 3 quart jars (1 L)

## Ingredients:

- 2.2 pounds (1 kg) carrots, peeled, sliced

- ½ tablespoon (7.5 ml) olive oil

- 1 tablespoon (15 g) salt

- ½ teaspoon (½ g) dried thyme

- ½ teaspoon (2.5 g) ground coriander

- ¼ teaspoon (1.25 g) ground cumin

- ½ tablespoon (7.5 ml) olive oil

- 1 teaspoon (5 g) onion powder

- ½ teaspoon (2.5 g) ground dried ginger

- ½ teaspoon (2.5 g) ground black pepper

- 1 ½ tablespoons (7.5 ml) bottled lemon juice

Serving instructions per serving 1 pint (500 ml) jar or quart (1 L) jar:

- Crème fraiche

- Maple syrup

**Directions:**

1. Arrange the pressure canner, canning lids, and jars. You need six 1 pint (500 ml) size jars or three quart size (1 L) jars. Pour enough water into the pressure canner following the manufacturer's instructions such that it is about 3 inches (8 centimeters) in height from the bottom of the canner. Place the canner on your stovetop over low heat. Place the jars in the canner so that the jars remain warm. The temperature of the water in the canner should be maintained at 180°F (82°C). Place the lids in a small saucepan of water over low heat on another burner.

2. Pour oil into a stock pot and heat the oil over high heat. Add fennel and carrot and sauté for a couple of minutes. Add the spices and salt and stir for about a minute. You will get a nice fragrance. Pour broth and let it start boiling. Lower the heat and let it simmer for a few minutes until tender. The vegetables are not to be fully cooked as they will cook further in the canning process. Turn off the heat.

3. Place the jars on a towel. Remove the vegetables from the stock pot with a slotted spoon and distribute them among the jars. Make sure the vegetables are equally distributed in the jars. Pour boiling broth into the jars to get 1 inch (2.5 cm) headspace.

4. Make sure to remove bubbles using a bubble removing tool. Reassess the headspace and add more boiling liquid if required to fill up to the required headspace.

5. Take a clean damp cloth and wipe the rim of the jars. Place the canning lid on each jar using the lid lifter. Place the canning ring on each jar and tighten it as suggested.

6. Place the jars in the canner and process the jars following the manufacturer's instruction manual at 10 psi (69 kPa). Set the timer for 40 minutes for 1 pint size (500 ml) jars or 50 minutes for quart (1L) size jars, adjusting for altitude if required. Once the timer goes off, turn off the burner.

7. Once you are done with the processing, let the pressure release naturally before opening the canner and taking out the jars. Let the jars cool completely on your countertop for no less than 12 hours. Wipe the jars with a dry kitchen cloth or paper towel. Make sure to check for the seals. These jars will last you for about 12 months.

8. **Serving instructions**: Empty the contents of a can into a blender and blend until smooth. Pour the soup into a saucepan and heat thoroughly. Combine some crème fraiche and maple syrup in a bowl. Ladle into soup bowls. Drizzle crème fraiche mixture on top and serve.

# Asparagus Soup

Makes: 8 pint jars (500 ml)

**Ingredients:**

- 6 pounds (2.7 kg) fresh asparagus

- 2 cups (320 g) minced shallots

- 1 teaspoon (5 g) salt

- 16 cups (4 L) chicken broth or stock

- Six large cloves garlic, minced

- ½ teaspoon (2.5 g) ground white pepper

- 1 tablespoon (15 ml) olive oil

Serving instructions per serving 1 pint (500 ml) jar:

- ¼ cup (62.5 ml) heavy cream

- Grated parmesan cheese to taste

- Salt and pepper to taste

**Directions:**

1. Trim the hard part of the stems from the asparagus and discard. Cut the asparagus into ½ inch (1.25 cm) pieces.

2. Pour oil into a pan and allow the oil to heat over medium heat. Add shallots and garlic and cook for a few minutes until soft, being careful not to cook them for too long. Boil broth in a pot.

3. Next arrange the pressure canner, canning lids, and jars. You need eight 1 pint (500 ml) size jars. Pour enough water into the pressure canner following the manufacturer's instructions such that it is about 3 inches (8 centimeters) in height from the bottom of the canner. Place the canner on your stovetop over low heat. Place the jars in the canner so that the jars remain warm. The temperature of the water in the canner should be maintained at 180°F (82°C). Place the lids in a small saucepan of water over low heat on another burner.

4. Place the jars on a towel. Place the funnel over the rim of the jar. Add asparagus pieces into the jars, filling up to ¾ the jars. Divide the shallot mixture among jars. Divide the salt and pepper among the jars.

5. Pour boiling broth into the jars until you get 1 inch (2.5 cm) headspace.

6. Make sure to remove bubbles using a bubble removing tool. Reassess the headspace and add more boiling liquid if required to fill up to the required headspace.

7. Take a clean damp cloth and wipe the rim of the jars. Place the canning lid on each jar using the lid lifter. Place the canning ring on each jar and tighten it as suggested.

8. Place the jars in the canner and process the jars following the manufacturer's instruction manual at 10 psi (69 kPa). Set the timer for 75 minutes for 1 pint size (500 ml) jars, adjusting for altitude if required. Once the timer goes off, turn off the burner.

9. Once you are done with the processing, let the pressure release naturally before opening the canner and taking out the jars. Let the jars cool completely on your countertop for no less than 12 hours. Wipe the jars with a dry kitchen cloth or paper towel. Make sure to check for the seals. These jars will last you for about 12 months.

10. **Serving suggestion**: Empty the contents of a jar into a saucepan. Place the saucepan over medium heat. Remove a few pieces of asparagus from the saucepan and keep it aside. Blend the asparagus in the saucepan with an immersion blender until pureed well. Add salt and pepper to taste. Add cream and let the cream blend well into the soup. When the soup is nice and hot, turn off the heat. Ladle the soup into bowls. Top with retained asparagus pieces and cheese and serve.

# Vegetable Soup

Makes: 6 pint jars (500 ml)

**Ingredients:**

- 2 ½ quarts (2.5 L) vegetable broth or chicken broth

- Four ears corn, use the kernels

- 12–15 green beans, cut into 1 inch pieces

- 1 cup (125 g) sliced celery

- Two cloves garlic, peeled**Error! Bookmark not defined.**, minced

- 2 cups (400 g) peeled, chopped tomatoes

- ½ pound (227 g) potatoes, peeled, cut into cubes

- One large carrot, sliced

- One medium onion, chopped

- ½ teaspoon (½ g) dried thyme, crushed

- ½ teaspoon (½ g) dried marjoram, crushed

- ½ teaspoon (½ g) dried parsley, crushed

- ½ teaspoon (½ g) dried rosemary, crushed

- Ground black pepper to taste

Serving instructions per serving 1 pint (500 ml) jar:

- 1 tablespoon cornstarch

- Chopped fresh herbs of your choice

- Grated cheese

**Directions:**

1. Arrange the pressure canner, canning lids, and jars. You need six 1 pint (500 ml) size jars. Pour enough water into the pressure canner following the manufacturer's instructions such that it is about 3 inches (8 centimeters) in height from the bottom of the canner. Place the canner on your stovetop over low heat. Place the jars in the canner so that the jars remain warm. The temperature of the water in the canner should be maintained at 180°F (82°C). Place the lids in a small saucepan of water over low heat on another burner.

2. Put the vegetables into a stock pot along with the stock, dried herbs and pepper. Place the pot over high heat. When the mixture starts boiling, reduce the heat and cover the

pot. Cook for 3-4 minutes. Turn off the heat. The vegetables should be crisp but not tender so do not cook for longer than 3 to 4 minutes. Turn off the heat.

3. Place the jars on a towel. Place the funnel over the rim of the jar. Remove vegetables with a slotted spoon and add into the jars, making sure each jar has an equal amount of vegetables.

4. Now pour the broth into the jars until you get 1 inch (2.5 cm) headspace.

5. Make sure to remove bubbles using a bubble removing tool. Reassess the headspace and add more boiling liquid if required to fill up to the required headspace.

6. Take a clean damp cloth and wipe the rim of the jars. Place the canning lid on each jar using the lid lifter. Place the canning ring on each jar and tighten it as suggested.

7. Place the jars in the canner and process the jars following the manufacturer's instruction manual at 10 psi (69 kPa). Set the timer for 60 minutes for 1 pint size (500 ml) jars, adjusting for altitude if required. Once the timer goes off, turn off the burner.

8. Once you are done with the processing, let the pressure release naturally before opening the canner and taking out the jars. Let the jars cool completely on your countertop for no less than 12 hours. Wipe the jars with a dry kitchen cloth or paper towel. Make sure to check for the seals. These jars will last you for about 12 months.

9. **Serving suggestion:** Take out a little of the broth from the jar and add into a bowl. Add cornstarch and whisk well. Empty the contents of a jar into a saucepan. Place the saucepan over medium heat. Add cornstarch mixture and keep stirring until the soup is thickened. Heat thoroughly. Ladle the soup into soup bowls. Garnish with herbs and parsley and serve.

# Tomato Soup

Makes: 8 pint jars (500 ml)

**Ingredients:**

- 16 pounds (7.3 kg) tomatoes

- Four medium onions, diced

- 12 bay leaves

- 1 teaspoon (5 g) ground black pepper

- ½ cup (100 g) sugar (optional)

- 2 cups (250 g) sliced**Error! Bookmark not defined.** celery

- 2 cups (110 g) chopped fresh parsley

- 1 ½ cups (375 ml) Clear Gel canning starch

- 5 tablespoons (75 g) salt or to taste (optional)

<u>Serving instructions per serving 1 pint (500 ml) jar:</u>
- 2 cups milk or water or broth

- Light cream

- Grated cheese

**Directions:**

1. Add tomatoes, onion, parsley, bay leaves, and parsley into a large stainless steel pot and place the pot over medium heat.

2. As it cooks, stir periodically so that the tomatoes do not get stuck on the bottom of the saucepan. Turn off the heat and spoon the mixture into a food mill or strainer in batches and strain the tomatoes. Discard the solids remaining in the food mill. Pour 4 cups of the strained mixture into a bowl and keep it aside to cool. Pour remaining soup into the pot.

3. Arrange the pressure canner, canning lids, and jars. You need eight 1 pint (500 ml) size jars. Pour enough water into the pressure canner following the manufacturer's instructions such that it is about 3 inches (8 centimeters) in height from the bottom of the canner. Place the canner on your stovetop over low heat. Place the jars in the canner so that the jars remain warm. The temperature of the water in the canner should be maintained at 180°F (82°C). Place the lids in a small saucepan of water over low heat on another burner.

4. Place the pot over medium-high heat. Let the soup start boiling. Once the puree cools, add clear gel and whisk well. Add into the pot. Stir constantly until the soup is thick. Add salt, pepper, and sugar and mix well. Keep stirring until sugar dissolves completely. Turn off the heat.

5.  Place the jars on a towel. Place the funnel over the rim of the jar. Now pour the soup into the jars until you get 1 inch (2.5 cm) headspace.

6.  Make sure to remove bubbles using a bubble removing tool. Reassess the headspace and add more boiling liquid if required to fill up to the required headspace.

7.  Take a clean damp cloth and wipe the rim of the jars. Place the canning lid on each jar using the lid lifter. Place the canning ring on each jar and tighten it as suggested.

8.  Place the jars in the canner and process the jars following the manufacturer's instruction manual at 10 psi (69 kPa). Set the timer for 25 minutes for 1 pint size (500 ml) jars, adjusting for altitude if required. Once the timer goes off, turn off the burner.

9.  Once you are done with the processing, let the pressure release naturally before opening the canner and taking out the jars. Let the jars cool completely on your countertop for no less than 12 hours. Wipe the jars with a dry kitchen cloth or paper towel. Make sure to check for the seals. These jars will last you for about 12 months.

10. **Serving suggestion**: Empty the contents of a jar into a saucepan. Add the chosen liquid and place the saucepan over medium heat. Stir often and bring the soup to a boil. Turn off the heat. Ladle the soup into bowls. Drizzle some cream on top. Garnish with cheese and serve.

# Mexican Beef Garden Soup

Makes: 9 pint jars (500 ml)

**Ingredients:**

- 1 tablespoon (15 ml) vegetable oil

- 2.5 quarts (2.5 L) low-sodium beef broth

- Four carrots about 1 inch (2.5 cm) diameter, cut into ¼ inch (0.6 cm) round slices

- 1 cup (174 g) fresh or frozen corn kernels

- Two Poblano chili pepper, discard stem and seeds, chopped

- Six cloves garlic, mined

- ½ tablespoon (7.5 g) chili powder

- 2.5 pounds (1.1 kg) beef chuck roast, trimmed of fat, cut into 1 inch (2.5 cm) chunks

- Four Roma tomatoes, deseeded, chopped

- One medium sweet potato, peeled, chopped

- 1 ½ medium onions, chopped

- 2 jalapeño peppers, deseeded, finely chopped

- 1 tablespoon (15 g) salt

- ½ tablespoon (7.5 g) ground black pepper

Serving instructions per serving 1 pint (500 ml) jar:
- Chopped avocado

- Chopped fresh cilantro

- Chopped red onions

- Tortilla chips, crumbled

- Squeeze of lemon juice

## Directions:

1. Pour oil into a large stock pot and let the pot heat over medium-high heat. When oil is hot, add beef and cook until brown all over.

2. Pour broth and scrape the bottom of the pot to remove any browned bits that may be stuck. When the soup starts boiling, lower the heat and cover with a lid. Let the meat cook until tender.

3. Meanwhile, arrange the pressure canner, canning lids, and jars. You need nine 1 pint (500 ml) size jars. Pour enough water into the pressure canner following the manufacturer's instructions such that it is about 3 inches (8 centimeters) in height from the bottom of the canner. Place the canner on your stovetop over low heat. Place the jars in the canner so that the jars remain warm. The temperature of the water in the canner should be maintained at 180°F (82°C). Place the lids in a small saucepan of water over low heat on another burner.

4. Once meat is tender, add all the spices and vegetables into the pot. When the mixture starts boiling, cover the pot with a lid and let it cook for five minutes. Turn off the heat.

5. Place the jars on a towel. Place the funnel over the rim of the jar. Remove vegetables and meat with a slotted spoon and add into the jars, making sure each jar has equal amounts of vegetables and meat. The jars would be about half filled with the vegetables and meat.

6. Now pour the broth into the jars until you get 1 inch (2.5 cm) headspace.

7. Make sure to remove bubbles using a bubble removing tool. Reassess the headspace and add more boiling liquid if required to fill up to the required headspace.

8. Take a clean damp cloth and wipe the rim of the jars. Place the canning lid on each jar using the lid lifter. Place the canning ring on each jar and tighten it as suggested.

9. Place the jars in the canner and process the jars following the manufacturer's instruction manual at 10 psi (69 kPa). Set the timer for 60 minutes for 1 pint size (500 ml) jars, adjusting for altitude if required. Once the timer goes off, turn off the burner.

10. Once you are done with the processing, let the pressure release naturally before opening the canner and taking out the jars. Let the jars cool completely on your countertop for no less than 12 hours. Wipe the jars with a dry kitchen cloth or paper towel. Make sure to check for the seals. These jars will last you for about 12 months.

11. **Serving suggestion**: Empty the contents of a jar into a saucepan. Place the saucepan over medium heat. Heat the soup thoroughly. Ladle the soup into soup bowls. Drizzle lemon juice on top. Top with avocado, onion, and cilantro. Finally top with tortilla chips and serve.

# Colorful Soup

Makes: 5 quart jars (1 L)

**Ingredients:**

- Five medium potatoes, peeled**Error! Bookmark not defined.**, cut into cubes (about 5 cups)

- 4 cups (696 g) corn kernels**Error! Bookmark not defined.**

- 2 ½ cups (370 g) cooked chicken, retain the broth in which chicken was cooked

- 2-3 fresh Roma tomatoes, chopped

- Five medium carrots, sliced (about 5 cups)

- 4 cups (696 g) sliced green beans

- One large onion, chopped

- 1 2/3 cups (242 g) green peas

- 2 ½ chicken bouillon cubes

Serving instructions per serving 1 quart (1 L) jar:

- Squeeze of lemon juice

- Chopped fresh herbs of your choice

**Directions:**

1. Arrange the pressure canner, canning lids, and jars. You need five quart size (1 L) jars. Pour enough water into the pressure canner following the manufacturer's instructions such that it is about 3 inches (8 centimeters) in height from the bottom of the canner. Place the canner on your stovetop over low heat. Place the jars in the canner so that the jars remain warm. The temperature of the water in the canner should be maintained at 180°F (82°C). Place the lids in a small saucepan of water over low heat on another burner.

2. Boil the chicken broth in a pot.

3. Place the jars on a towel. Place the funnel over the rim of the jar. Place the vegetables and chicken in the jars in layers, making sure to distribute the ingredients equally. Make it colorful. You can place alternate layers of dark and light colored vegetables and chicken and make it look colorful.

4. Now pour the broth into the jars until you get 1 inch (2.5 cm) headspace.

5. Make sure to remove bubbles using a bubble removing tool. Reassess the headspace and add more boiling liquid if required to fill up to the required headspace.

6. Take a clean damp cloth and wipe the rim of the jars. Place the canning lid on each jar using the lid lifter. Place the canning ring on each jar and tighten it as suggested.

7. Place the jars in the canner and process the jars following the manufacturer's instruction manual at 10 psi (69 kPa). Set the timer for 90 minutes for quart size (1 L) jars, adjusting for altitude if required. Once the timer goes off, turn off the burner.

8. Once you are done with the processing, let the pressure release naturally before opening the canner and taking out the jars. Let the jars cool completely on your countertop for no less than 12 hours. Wipe the jars with a dry kitchen cloth or paper towel. Make sure to check for the seals. These jars will last you for about 12 months.

9. **Serving suggestion**: Empty the contents of a jar into a saucepan. Place the saucepan over medium heat. Heat the soup thoroughly. Ladle the soup into bowls. Drizzle some lemon juice on top. Garnish with fresh herbs on top and serve.

# Chile, Corn, and Chicken Chowder

Makes: 10 quart jars (1 L)

**Ingredients:**

- 4 tablespoons (60 ml) vegetable oil

- 2 cups (250 g) sliced celery

- 4 teaspoons ground Ancho chili pepper or mild chili powder

- 10 cups (1.74 kg) fresh corn kernels

- Freshly ground black pepper to taste

- Six medium onions, chopped

- Four Poblano chili peppers, deseeded, chopped

- 6 quarts (6 L) low-sodium chicken broth

Serving instructions per serving 1 quart (1 L) jar:

- ½ cup instant mashed potato flakes

- American cheese slices

**Directions:**

1. Arrange the pressure canner, canning lids, and jars. You need 10 quart size (1 L) jars. Pour enough water into the pressure canner following the manufacturer's instructions such that it is about 3 inches (8 centimeters) in height from the bottom of the canner. Place the canner on your stovetop over low heat. Place the jars in the canner so that the jars remain warm. The temperature of the water in the canner should be maintained at 180°F (82°C). Place the lids in a small saucepan of water over low heat on another burner.

2.  Pour oil into a large stock pot and let the pot heat over medium-high heat. When oil is hot, drop the onions, chilies, and celery into the pot and cook for a few minutes until onions are pink. Add chili powder and mix well.

3.  Stir in chicken, broth, black pepper, and corn. When the mixture starts boiling, turn off the heat.

4.  Place the jars on a towel. Place the funnel over the rim of the jar. Remove the vegetables and chicken with a slotted spoon and place in the jars.

5.  Now pour the broth into the jars until you get 1 inch (2.5 cm) headspace. In case you are short of broth, boil some more broth or water and add.

6.  Make sure to remove bubbles using a bubble removing tool. Reassess the headspace and add more boiling liquid if required to fill up to the required headspace.

7.  Take a clean damp cloth and wipe the rim of the jars. Place the canning lid on each jar using the lid lifter. Place the canning ring on each jar and tighten it as suggested.

8.  Place the jars in the canner and process the jars following the manufacturer's instruction manual at 10 psi (69 kPa). Set the timer for 75 minutes for quart size (1 L) jars, adjusting for altitude if required. Once the timer goes off, turn off the burner.

9.  Once you are done with the processing, let the pressure release naturally before opening the canner and taking out the jars. Let the jars cool completely on your countertop for no less than 12 hours. Wipe the jars with a dry kitchen cloth or paper towel. Make sure to check for the seals. These jars will last you for about 12 months.

10. **Serving suggestion**: Empty the contents of a jar into a saucepan. Place the saucepan over medium heat. Cover the saucepan and let it heat for about 10 minutes. Turn off the heat. Stir in instant mashed potato flakes. Tear up a couple of slices of cheese and add into the soup. Mix well. Once cheese melts, ladle into soup bowls and serve.

# Appendix 1 – Altitude in USA Cities & Canadian Cities

**Chart of the 20 largest cities in the U.S. and their Altitudes**

| City | State | Altitude | Rank by population |
|------|-------|----------|--------------------|
| Phoenix | Arizona | 1086 ft | 5 |
| Denver | Colorado | 948 ft | 19 |
| Columbus | Ohio | 902 ft | 15 |
| Charlotte | North Carolina | 761 ft | 16 |
| Indianapolis | Indiana | 719 ft | 17 |
| Fort Worth | Texas | 653 ft | 13 |
| San Antonio | Texas | 650 ft | 7 |
| Chicago | Illinois | 597 ft | 3 |
| Dallas | Texas | 430 ft | 9 |
| Austin | Texas | 425 ft | 11 |
| Washington | D.C. | 409 ft | 20 |
| Los Angeles | California | 305 ft | 2 |
| Seattle | Washington | 174 ft | 18 |

| | | | |
|---|---|---|---|
| Houston | Texas | 105 ft | 4 |
| San Jose | California | 82 ft | 10 |
| San Diego | California | 62 ft | 8 |
| San Francisco | California | 52 ft | 14 |
| Philadelphia | Pennsylvania | 39 ft | 6 |
| New York City | New York | 33 ft | 1 |
| Jacksonville | Florida | 16 ft | 12 |

## 5 cities with the highest altitudes in the U.S.

| City | State | Altitude |
|---|---|---|
| Alma | Colorado | 10,361 ft |
| Leadville | Colorado | 10,150 ft |
| Blue River | Colorado | 10,020 ft |
| Breckenridge | Colorado | 9,600 ft |
| Flagstaff | Arizona | 6,910 ft |

## Altitude of the 10 largest cities in Canada

| City | Province | Altitude | Rank by population |
|------|----------|----------|--------------------|
| Vancouver, | British Columbia | 6,562 ft | 8 |
| Calgary | Alberta | 3,428 ft | 3 |
| Edmonton | Alberta | 2,116 ft | 5 |
| Hamilton | Ontario | 1083 ft | 10 |
| Winnipeg | Manitoba | 784 ft | 7 |
| Montreal | Quebec | 764 ft | 2 |
| Brampton | Ontario | 715 ft | 9 |
| Mississauga | Ontario | 512 ft | 6 |
| Toronto | Ontario | 251 ft | 1 |
| Ottawa | Ontario | 230 ft | 4 |

# Appendix 2 - Measurement Conversion

| Cups | Tablespoons | Teaspoons | Milliliters |
|------|-------------|-----------|-------------|
|  |  | 1 tsp | 5 ml |
| 1/16 cups | 1 tbsp | 3 tsp | 15 ml |
| ⅛ cups | 2 tbsp | 6 tsp | 30 ml |
| ¼ cups | 4 tbsp | 12 tsp | 60 ml |
| ⅓ cups | 5 ⅓ tbsp | 16 tsp | 80 ml |
| ½ cups | 8 tbsp | 24 tsp | 120 ml |
| ⅔ cups | 10 ⅔ tbsp | 32 tsp | 160ml |
| ¾ cups | 12 tbsp | 36 tsp | 180 ml |
| 1 cup | 16 tbsp | 48 tsp | 240 ml |

1 Gallon = 4 quarts = 8 pints =16 cups= 120 oz = 3.8 liters

1 Quart = 2 pints= 4 cups = 32 oz = 950 ml

1 Pint = 2 cups= 16 oz = 480 ml

1 cup = 8oz= 240ml

## Cooking Temperatures

Fahrenheit = (Celsius x 1.8) +32

Celsius = (Fahrenheit - 32) x 0.5556

## Pounds to Kilograms

| | |
|---|---|
| 1 lb = 0.45 kg | 1 kg= 2.22 lbs |
| 2 lbs = 0.90 kg | 2 kg= 4.44 lbs |
| 3 lbs = 1.35 kg | 3 kg= 6.67 lbs |
| 4lbs = 1.80 kg | 4 kg= 8.89 lbs |
| 5 lbs = 2.25 kg | 5 kg= 11.11 lbs |
| 6 lbs = 2.70 kg | 6 kg= 13.33lbs |
| 7 lbs = 3.15 kg | 7 kg= 15.56 lbs |
| 8 lbs = 3.60 kg | 8 kg= 17.78 lbs |
| 9 lbs = 4.05 kg | 9 kg= 20.00 lbs |
| 10 lbs = 4.50 kg | 10 kg= 22.22 lbs |

# Conclusion

"Laughter is brightest where food is best."

In this book, you were introduced to all the information you need about canning. Before you start, it is important that you take time to learn about the USDA guidelines for safe canning and how your pressure canner works. Learning about the different parts of the pressure canner will give you a better understanding of pressure canning. Knowing this makes a lot of difference when it comes to the results obtained while using a specific recipe. You were also introduced to different types of pressure canner and how they work. After this, the tools and equipment you will need to start canning at home were also described. By now, you might have realized that pressure canning is easier than you believed. Once you start following the step-by-step process described, you can get brilliant results every single time.

You should also make it a point to develop a few practices to ensure high-quality results. Whether it is strictly following a recipe, cleanliness protocols while canning, or handling the pressure canner, best practices for safety and so on. Also, these practices ensure you get high-quality results. When it comes to food safety, it is always better to err on the side of caution. Always listen to the recipe, but first make sure it aligns with the USDA's food protocols. Do not forget to adjust the temperature and pressure according to altitude. Also make it a point that you always focus on the acidity of the ingredients used too.

You were also introduced to different recipes you can use to start canning at home. Whether it is beef, pork, turkey, or wild game, the sky's the limit when it comes to canning. Once you've become comfortable with your pressure canner, feel free to be creative. Don't forget to try different vegetarian and vegan-friendly food options as well. Canning is easy once you have all the tools and equipment needed along with the correct ingredients. After this, you simply need to follow the instructions given in the recipe of your choice and start canning! Once you get the hang of it, you can enjoy your favorite food with your loved ones all year long.

Thank you and all the best!

# Thank You

Dear reader, I would like to take this time to appreciate you.

Without your purchase and interest, I wouldn't be able to keep writing helpful books like this one.

Once again, THANK YOU for reading this book. I hope you enjoyed it as much as I enjoyed writing it.

Before you go, I have a small favor to ask of you. **Would you please consider posting a review of this book on the platform? Posting a review will help support my writing as an independent author.**

Your feedback is very important and will help me continue to provide more informative literature in the future. I look forward to hearing from you.

## >> Leave a review on Amazon US <<

## >> Leave a review on Amazon CA <<

## >> Leave a review on Amazon UK <<

## >> Leave a review on Amazon AUS <<

Lastly, if interested, please click the link below to visit my author page on Amazon to see my other books on Food Preservation.

Linda.

## >> Click here to see my other books on Food Preservation <<

# References

Andress, E. (2014). *Preserving food: Using pressure canners.* National Center for Home Food Preservation | UGA Publications. https://nchfp.uga.edu/publications/uga/using_press_canners.html

Chihaak, S. (2020, April 6). *Master pressure canning at home in 9 simple steps.* Better Homes & Gardens. https://www.bhg.com/recipes/how-to/preserving-canning/pressure-canning-basics/

HGIC 3030. (2011, August 20). *Canning foods—the pH factor.* Home & Garden Information Center | Clemson University, South Carolina. Https://hgic.clemson.edu/factsheet/canning-foods-the-pH-factor/#:~:text=The%20acidity%2C%20or%20pH%2C%20of,processed%20in%20a%20pressure%20canner.

Homestead Dreamer. (2016, October 10). *Unraveling the mystery: Water bath vs pressure canning.* Homestead Dreamer. Http://www.homesteaddreamer.com/2016/10/10/water-bath-vs-pressure-canning/

Kring, L. (2016, July 23). *13 top tips for successful pressure canning.* Foodal. https://foodal.com/knowledge/things-that-preserve/tips-home-canning/

Meredith, L. (2020, September 17). *Boiling water bath and pressure canning - When to use which.* The Spruce Eats. https://www.thespruceeats.com/boiling-water-bath-versus-pressure-canning-1327438

Mountain Feed & Farm Supply. (n.d.). *Our must-have list of canning equipment & supplies.* Mountain Feed & Farm Supply. Https://www.mountainfeed.com/blogs/learn/15522713-our-must-have-list-of-canning-equipment-supplies

Penn State Extension. (n.d.). *Time, temperature, pressure in canning foods.* Penn State Extension. Https://extension.psu.edu/time-temperature-pressure-in-canning-foods

Peterson, S. (2020, April 11). *What is botulism?* SimplyCanning. Https://www.simplycanning.com/botulism/

Peterson, S. (2021, October 7). *Pressure canners: The brands, features, and how they work!* SimplyCanning. Https://www.simplycanning.com/pressure-canner/#pressurecanner3

# Images References

Anshu. (n.d.). *Tomato sauce* [Unsplash]. https://unsplash.com/photos/mVUs_adTiX8

Brown, M. (n.d.). *Pressure dial gauge* [Pixabay]. https://pixabay.com/photos/pressure-gauge-gauge-pressure-5156070/

Cala. (n.d.). *Carrot soup* [Unsplash]. https://unsplash.com/photos/w6ftFbPCs9I

Castrejon, E. (n.d.). *Canned dried beans* [Unsplash]. https://unsplash.com/photos/1SPu0KT-Ejg

Didier. (n.d.). *Tomato sauce* [Pixabay]. https://pixabay.com/users/mrdidg-11821588/

Dmitriy. (n.d.). *Canned baked beans* [Pixabay]. https://pixabay.com/photos/vegetarian-white-canned-bean-5029296/

Doan, V. (n.d.). *Green beans* [Pixabay]. https://pixabay.com/photos/green-bean-food-green-healthy-1443290/

Kalhh. (n.d.). *Chili con carne* [Pixabay]. https://pixabay.com/photos/chili-con-carne-chili-cook-378952/

Licht-aus. (n.d.). *Food strainer* [Pixabay]. https://pixabay.com/photos/sock-strainer-banana-chopsticks-6316925/

Mona. (n.d.). *Asparagus soup* [Pixabay]. https://pixabay.com/photos/soup-asparagus-green-colour-2649392/

Merkman, K. (n.d.). *Tin can vessel* [Pixabay]. https://pixabay.com/vectors/tin-can-vessel-disposal-metal-3778762/

Myriam. (n.d.). *Ratatouille* [Pixabay]. https://pixabay.com/photos/ratatouille-dish-food-vegetables-6498448/

Owen-Wahl, R. (n.d.). *Corned beef and potatoes* [Pixabay]. https://pixabay.com/photos/beef-food-peas-plate-snack-lunch-1238623/

Rivas, H. (n.d.). *Canned food* [Unsplash]. https://unsplash.com/photos/N7M7mSgUgwo

Schwarzenberger, M. (n.d.). *Pressure regulator* [Pixabay]. https://pixabay.com/photos/oxygen-pressure-regulator-502887/

Shaw, C. (n.d.). *Canned sausages* [Unsplash]. https://unsplash.com/photos/dR4Ab6-fH6M

Shrewberry, R. (n.d.). *Canned food* [Unsplash]. https://unsplash.com/photos/bhni1zsPiio

Tant, P. (n.d.). *Tomato soup* [Pixabay]. https://pixabay.com/photos/pepper-soup-tomato-soup-soup-food-1234763/

Thrainer, R. (n.d.). *Herbed potatoes* [Pixabay]. https://pixabay.com/photos/roasted-potatoes-rosemary-herbs-6568342/

Vittoriosi, E. (n.d.). *Asian turkey meatballs* [Unsplash]. https://unsplash.com/photos/OFismyezPnY

Made in United States
Orlando, FL
26 February 2023

30404339R00091